city squares of the world

© 2007 White Star s.p.a.
Via Candido Sassone, 22/24
13100 Vercelli, Italy
www.whitestar.it

TRANSLATION: ANGELA ARNONE

ISBN: 978-88-544-0276-8

REPRINT
1 2 3 4 5 6   11 10 09 08 07

Color separation: Fotomec, Turin
Printed in Indonesia

city squares of the world

text by Maria Teresa Feraboli

WHITE STAR PUBLISHERS

TEXT

by MARIA TERESA FERABOLI

Editorial Director

VALERIA MANFERTO DE FABIANIS

Editorial Coordinator

FEDERICA ROMAGNOLI

Graphic Designer

CLARA ZANOTTI

Graphic Layout

MARIA CUCCHI

5 ■ Piazza del Campidoglio, Rome, with its complex, elegant paving.

7 ■ The futuristic steel and glass cupola at the Sony Center, in Berlin's Potsdamer Platz.

10-11 ■ Saint Sophia and the Sultanahmet Meidani, a green lung in the heart of Istanbul.

12-13 ■ Ice-skaters in Nathan Phillips Square, Toronto.

CONTENTS

Introduction

Four continental regions – Europe, America, Asia, and Oceania – are the locations for the forty-some city squares selected for this book, and celebrated by it, with the intention s of illustrating the evolution of the urban square from the Middle Ages, when the concept assumed

"specialized" features that depended on its final purpose, to the present. In the most consolidated historiographical studies, the square's architectural theme is linked to its urban dimension in the Italian Renaissance, subsequently establishing several typological models in France that are still being applied today. Subsequently the square spread throughout Europe in the period that linked the Baroque to the Neoclassical era, before being exported to other continents.

The epitome of public and collective space, the square gradually became the expression of municipal freedom, of religious power wielded by the Church, of mercantile trade, and of royal celebrations for monarchs and government events. Up to the nineteenth-century, with its vast changes in social structure and urban fabric, the plaza thus evolved to the point of undertaking new functions and renewing the old: from garden squares to those conceived as road junctions, now flanked by new places for social gathering, like shopping arcades with impressive glass roofs, and other such centers that competed with open-air squares for the traditional role of providing a place for social intercourse and the personal rendezvous.

In the first half of the twentieth century, especially in Italy, the square re-established its significance as a civic space and pivotal point for organization of the urban nucleus in newly-built towns, while the urban planning ideals of the Modern Movement, as it was known, ratified by the Charter of Athens in 1933, enjoyed rather limited application. Following more recent trends, this period of the past is considered the conclusion of a cycle that had originated with the social and urban area changes that came about in the 1900s. This guided the decision to divide the book into two sections: one centering around the evolution of the square from its origins to the twentieth century, and the other dedicated to its reinterpretation, after the Second World War up to the present day, typified by the eclectic pragmatism so widespread in the era of multimedia communication.

Following post-war reconstruction, the profound ethical crisis in European Modernism gave way to the recovered valuation of the historical town, incarnated by schemes to upgrade existing squares, restore their role as meeting point and respite from the bustle of daily life and from vehicle traffic. Moreover, the creation of completely new spaces in the old fabric (Plateau Beaubourg, Paris) or in run-down areas (Plaça dels Països Catalans, Barcelona), confirmed the desire to revive the plaza as one of the Western World's greatest anthropological expressions, as it has been described, by exploring its potential through the lens of contemporary social demands.

Further confirmation of the importance attributed to this urban space is the fact that about one quarter of the squares described in this volume are part of UNESCO's World Heritage List, either independently – as is the case of plazas in Bremen, Brussels, Nancy and Moscow – or because they are within specifically protected areas, like the old centers of Siena, Florence, Rome, Venice, Prague, Mexico City, Istanbul, Budapest and Brasilia. Thus the square continues to be the great stone archive of the community. If its historical meaning is the stratified evidence of the passing of centuries, the material proof of secular, religious and artistic expressions of a population, then even today, through new configurations, it can offer a suitable interpretation of the changing social relations in the era of globalization.

from its ORIGINS
to the TWENTIETH CENTURY

The direct forerunner of the plaza, seen as an expression of
a community's civic rights, can be identified in the Greek *agorà*
and the Roman *forum*; in other words, the places where the chief
functions of public life were performed in Classical antiquity.

The *agorà* was the fulcrum of urban political and business life. It began as a formless space in which the most important structure was the *stoà*, a colonnaded portico, and acquired a uniform conformation in the Hellenistic period, concurrently with the overall design of the urban grid, initiated in 466 AD by Hippodamos of Miletus, who used an orthogonal layout. The Roman *forum*, whose plan is described by Vitruvius in his *De Architectura*, replaced the Greek *agorà* and was set where the main east-west street, or *decumanus*, encountered the main north-west street, the *cardo*. It was where the market was held but was also ringed by sacred buildings and tribunals, which made it the center of religious and secular life.

The clear-cut distinction between lay, ecclesiastical, and commercial power in the Middle Ages meant that the square became their embodiment – developing in close conjunction with municipal buildings and cathedrals inside the urban fabric – or it was installed at the municipal gates to facilitate trade. Significant examples are Piazza del Campo (Siena), Grand-Place (Brussels), Piazza dei Miracoli (Pisa). These "specializations," in some cases overlapping with one another, were delimited in scope by definition, as the "civic square," the "religious square" and the "market square," which continue to exist today, enriched with further functions that derive from civil and cultural transformations in society.

From the fifteenth century, when the Italian Renaissance began to flourish, a new period of studies and research began into proportion and geometry, which translated into the design of ideal towns, and which were reflected by existing centers and on the layout of the city square itself, whose architectural dimensions were linked to the urban scale. Michelangelo's refurbishment of Piazza del Campidoglio, preceded by the construction of Piazza Pio II in Pienza, is a model that still inspires architects in this regard: see Arata Isozaki's Tsukuba Center Square. Architecture and urban planning fused into a unity that was the prelude to the scenographic trends typical of the Baroque period, with the introduction of urban furnishings like fountains and sculptures to enhance the square, making it a stage where everyday life was enacted, like in Rome's Pizza Navona.

From top to bottom ▪ Piazza dei Miracoli, Pisa; Piazza Pio II, Pienza; Covent Garden, London; Piazza del Popolo, Rome; Piazza del Plebiscito, Naples; Königsplatz, Munich; Piazza Duomo, Milan; Piazza della Vittoria, Brescia.

On the heels of the Italian exploration came the French contribution, which pinpointed a new "specialization," generating an out-and-out typology: *the place royale*, whose prototype can be seen in what is now Place des Vosges. The *place royale* comprised a geometrical outline – founded on a rectangle, a triangle or a semicircle – with an equestrian statue of the sovereign in the center, surrounded by terraces of buildings expressed in regular modules, destined to be used as private homes. A successful model that nowadays translates into the postmodern emphasis is Montpellier's Place du Nombre d'Or, designed by Ricardo Bofill; it has its historical equivalent in the English *square*, with Inigo Jones's Covent Garden plaza normally indicated as the first example of the latter. In point of fact, this particular typology was popular even into the following century, enriched with a new measure of Neoclassicism that endowed its architectural projects with rigor and austerity.

The industrial revolution and the modification to the working and social structure brought a radical transformation of the urban layout, which extended, doing away with town walls and erecting buildings that imitated historical styles, opening new streets in the existing road network: squares became crossroads to handle the increasing amounts of vehicle traffic, and were added to stations, the real gateways of the 19th century metropolis, and a new dimension which, in the light of the subsequent failure of Modern Movement zoning principles, generated urban planning issues that are still relevant today.

PIAZZA DEL
CAMPO

[SIENA ■ ITALY]

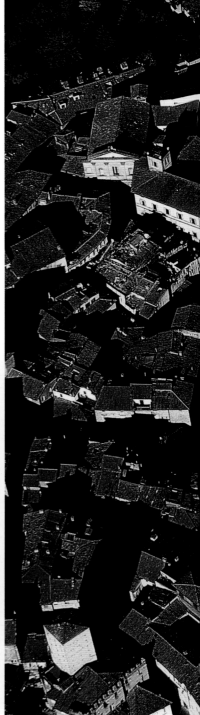

Piazza del Campo, better known as "il Campo" by the people of Siena, is one of the most beautiful, if not the most fascinating, of Italy's medieval squares. It is an urban space where it is still possible to sense the spirit that animated and inflamed the souls of Siena's citizens, united as they were in their praise of communal freedom, and prepared to defend their right to it, even if the only surviving traces of that civic passion are in the pugnacious attitude displayed during the famous Palio race. Documents of the time called the *statuti* describe a square with a lovely shell-valve configuration that in 1262 had two sectors: the Campus Fori, or marketplace, and the Campo di San Paolo, the higher area of what is now the *cavea* – a place for spectators.

In a later phase of urban development, the need arose to unite this space; and given the result obtained, several historians assert that it was the genius of Giovanni Pisano, who worked on the Duomo from 1284 to 1295, that made the city's main public space into one entity. The municipal authorities were always willing to contribute to the decoration of the square, to the point that numerous dispositions were issued to define the architectural features for the buildings facing the piazza, as well as strict regulations "policing" the activities and performances held there. For instance, the 1297 statutes provided that two-light windows would be inserted in any newly-erected buildings facing onto the Campo.

Development of the square continued with the purchase of private buildings, until the installation of brick paving, in about 1346. The pavement is divided into nine sectors by strips of gray stone, which converge from the upper part of the square towards the center of Palazzo Civico, and are an unmistakable reference to the nine governors then

in power in the city. In 1343 the Fonte Gaia was built, supplied by the network of underground channels called *bottini*, and in 1345 an aqueduct was installed. From 1409 to 1419, Jacopo della Quercia sculpted the figures that decorated the square until 1868, when they were removed to protect them from further corrosion, and replaced with copies by Tito Sarrocchi. The original marble panels have been placed on display in the Palazzo Civico.

The municipal building and the square were built practically at the same time and are not only closely connected but also dependent on the other, allowing the city's judiciary to have its own seat and the citizens to have a place suitable for assembly. The construction of the Palazzo Civico was the first example of a public secular building in the city and is said to have been designed by Agostino di Duccio, the master builder of the Duomo. Construction began in the late thirteenth century and included the building of the main block, proceeding swiftly as the need arose. By 1310 the Campo's side wings were more or less finished, and the overall appearance of the Palazzo as we know now it began to emerge with a higher central area, two lower side wings, to which a storey was added in 1680, and the underpinning for Torre del Mangia, the tower begun in 1325. The building of the Cappella di Piazza a chapel designed by Domenico di Agostino as a votive offering, followed a 1348 plague epidemic.

16 left ■ Vincenzo Rustici's painting, dating from 16th-17th century, portrays the procession to celebrate the Palio in Siena.

16-17 ■ The aerial view shows the conch shape, sloping down towards Palazzo Civico, which has made Piazza del Campo famous worldwide. The curtain of buildings on the opposite side from the Palazzo, crossed by eight streets, appears almost unbroken and surrounds the entire space.

LOCATION	YEAR OF CONSTRUCTION	AREA	APPLICATION	STYLE
SIENA (ITALY)	13TH-14TH CENTURY	APPROXIMATELY 118,400 SQ FEET	CIVIC SQUARE	GOTHIC

Today, the Campo preserves its historical shell layout, sloping down towards the Palazzo Civico and accessible from eight different streets that cut through the curved section of the constructions. They enter the perimeter paved in gray stone, and delimit the nine brick-paved sectors laid in a herringbone pattern. Another four streets enter the lower side, flanking either side of the Palazzo Civico. One of these, Via Salicotto, leads to the Cappella di Piazza, the marble loggia whose pillars – decorated with lancet arch aedicules containing statues of saints – support older Renaissance round arches. Behind it rises the massive silhouette of the municipal building, a majestic backdrop with slightly curved wings that adapt to the square's outline.

The presence of symmetrical blocks next to the main body, the curving, the base finished in stone and the upper part in brick, imply a closer relationship with the palazzo than with the fortress, as in the case of the contemporary Palazzo della Signoria in Florence. The ground floor includes a series of lancet arches, whereas the first and second floors open

18-19 and 20-21 ■ The square's paving is laid in a herringbone design, set in nine triangular sectors, separated by small marble pillars, which lead into the perimeter paved in grey stone, where the Palio race is run.

into a series of Gothic three-light windows. Two two-light windows, the "monogram of Bernardino," and a series of hanging arches enliven the third level of the central part, finished by flat-top merlons also found on the side wings. The slim, elegant Torre del Mangia emerges, off-center, from the wing behind the Piazza chapel, with a brick face and stone corbel coping.

Turning toward the opposite face of the municipal building, there is the Fonte Gaia, a rectangular fountain in the central part of the square. The Palazzo Sansedoni to its right was created in the eighteenth century by restructuring five buildings, and is lit by three orders of three-light Gothic windows; on the left is the Palazzo d'Elci, which retained its flat-top merlons despite refurbishing in the seventeenth century. Consequently, the square has retained, without alteration, the architectural harmony planned and given to it in the Middle Ages, making it one of the most successful and admired examples of a civic square anywhere.

PIAZZA DELLA
SIGNORIA

[FLORENCE ■ ITALY]

The origins of Piazza della Signoria are attributable to the dramatic Guelf-Ghibelline conflicts that bloodied Florence in the Thirteenth Century, when the victorious Guelfs destroyed the towers built by their adversaries, which were concentrated in this vicinity of the city.. They further decreed that no new building could be erected on that "damned terrain," which is how the open space that later became the piazza was originally created. In the meantime, the city's new authorities decided to erect a new public building.

The decision to build Palazzo dei Priori – now Palazzo Vecchio – came to fruition in 1299, when the first stone was laid, surrounding the existing Guardaboschi tower in a vast new complex most probably conceived by Arnolfo di Cambio, who was then active at the nearby Piazza del Duomo. Vasari writes that in his stubborn refusal to use the terrain that had housed the

22-23 ■ Piazza della Signoria's open space contrasts with the condensed volume of Palazzo Vecchio, designed by Arnolfo di Cambio in pietra forte stone, and finished with flat-top merlons.

23 top ■ The monumental Neptune fountain, by Bartolomeo Ammannati and his assistants, was placed near the Palazzo Vecchio to commemorate construction of an aqueduct. The colossal marble statue of Neptune is nicknamed "il Biancone" (white giant) by the Florentines because of its might.

23 bottom ■ A copy of Michelangelo's masterpiece, the David, next to Palazzo Vecchio. Behind it a glimpse of the Marzocco lion, the symbol of Florence, whose name derives from the god Mars; Donatello's original is in the Bargello Museum.

Uberti – a Ghibelline family – home, Arnolfo was forced to position the building "not aligned" but in asymmetrical relation to the square, nonetheless achieving what is still a highly admired result.

The piazza and the palazzo have always been inextricably linked, and the events that led to the construction of one modified the form of the other: it was the progressive demolitions of adjacent structures to extend the palazzo that gave the square its current appearance, characterized as it is by two sectors, at right angles to one another, making an L shape. Following the realization of the Uffizi, a perspective was opened over the River Arno, and what was to become Piazza della Signoria, which had been closed up to that time, acquired a greater scenic impact, further enhanced by the construction of the Loggia dei Priori and the inclusion of the statues that made the piazza a splendid open-air museum.

Palazzo Vecchio was completed in 1315, when Arnolfo's asymmetrical towering masterpiece had already been completed for several years, rising slightly to the right of the building's powerful stone mass – tall (300 feet), slim, and seemingly fragile, but actually extremely solid as it is the continuation of the previous, englobed tower. As soon as the Priori premises were

LOCATION	YEAR OF CONSTRUCTION	AREA	APPLICATION	STYLE
FLORENCE (ITALY)	13TH-14TH CENTURY	APPROXIMATELY 64,600 SQ FEET	CIVIC SQUARE	GOTHIC

completed, the piazza became the fulcrum of Florentine political power; separate from the religious seat of power in the Duomo site, though joined directly to it by Via dei Calzaiuoli.

As the piazza's importance grew, city authorities retained their commitment to completing the embellishment of the site, which had by then become a symbol of the city itself: in 1359 the Tribunale della Mercanzia building was erected at the corner of Via de' Gondi; and between 1376 and 1382, the Loggia della Signoria, designed by Orcagna but actually built by Benci di Cione and Simone Talenti, was constructed as a venue for public assembles and ceremonies. (Oddly, it was only in the Nineteenth Century that the piazza was given an official name. Until then it was identified with the Priors, who crossed it each day to reach the building that had emerged on the mound of ruins left by the destruction of the Ghibelline towers.)

When the Republic fell, the piazza's function changed: First Duke Alessandro I de' Medici used it as a barracks for the Landsknecht troops, which caused the Loggia to be known disparagingly as "dei Lanzi"; then Cosimo I set up an artist's workshop there, and it gradually became a studio or gallery of sorts. The piazza's appearance changed little, apart from the demolition of the Loggia dei Pisani, which had been built by prisoners taken in 1343 during the war against Pisa. It was replaced in the Nineteenth Century with a construction led by Assicurazioni Generali. In 1980, another restoration included the complete reinstatement of the *pietra serena* sandstone flooring.

24-25 ■ The Loggia dei Lanzi, covered with cross vaults on sandstone columns, houses numerous sculptures, with Giambologna's marble "Rape of the Sabines" clearly visible in the foreground.

Today the far left of the Palazzo Vecchio stairs is home to a copy of Donatello's *pietra serena* sandstone "Marzocco," Florence's iconic lion, whose name is derived from Mars, who it displaced in the city's insignia. Slightly to the right there is another Donatello copy, the bronze of Judith and Holophernes with an inscription declaring the intention of recovering republican freedom, installed here after the expulsion of Piero de' Medici in 1495. On the right of the Palazzo entrance is a copy of Michelangelo's David, a symbol of the victory of democracy over tyranny. On the opposite side, the David is balanced by Baccio Bandinelli's marble group of Hercules and Cacus, commissioned by the Medici family on their return to Florence, as the emblem of their victory over the domestic enemy. On the Loggia dei Lanzi, Cellini's Perseus stands up proudly against David and Judith and Holophernes.

Two monuments of minor artistic standing are an integral part of the of the piazza: the equestrian statue of Cosimo I, on the main axis leading to Via de' Cerchi, by Giambologna, and Ammannati's Neptune fountain, the "Biancone," which was also erected to celebrate Cosimo I and is located next to Palazzo Vecchio. In front of the fountain an epigraph commemorates the place where Girolamo Savonarola was burned at the stake in 1498. Notwithstanding the replacement of the sculptures for their preservation, Piazza della Signoria is still a mandatory destination for throngs of entranced Italians and tourists from abroad.

26 top ■ The Late Baroque
church of St. Nicholas is
the work of Kilian Ignaz
Dientzenhofer, who also designed
the Kinsky´ mansion, on the
opposite side of the square,
and was built by Anselmo Lurago.

STAROMĚSTSKÉ
NÁMĚSTÍ

[PRAGUE ■ CZECH REPUBLIC]

Staroměstské Náměstí, known in English as Prague's Old Town Square, astounds and fa-
scinates visitors not only for its unique features, but also because it does not meet any
established tenet of urban planning. This is one of Europe's most eclectic public spaces,
encapsulating almost every style of architecture from Gothic to Late Baroque. Astonis-
hingly, it does not reflect a Romanesque presence, which one would expect, considering
the sheer age of the settlements in the area. Nevertheless, recent archaeological and
architectural work on the cellars of the buildings that line the square has revealed important traces of the period. As well as bringing to light an early Gothic construction in
the patrician Volfin house, found at what is now the corner of City Hall tower, other re-
lics came from the Al Gallo House and the Týn School, dated mid-thirteenth century. The
disappearance of traces dating back to the Dark Ages is explainable: as the Middle Ages
drew to a close, the street level was raised by means of embankments to prevent floo-

ding by the Vltava, which regularly devastated the Old Town. The history of the square, which is the heart of the Old Town, is thus over 1000 years old and linked to the history of castle, which was begun in the ninth century by Prince Borivoj. Settlements that arose around the manor-house, set on a hillock on the left bank of the Vltava, stretched over the right bank from the eleventh century onward, forming the area around today's square. Originally this was a marketplace, but after City Hall was built, in 1338, it became a theater for dramatic political events that included the 1621 execution of nobles who headed a Protestant revolt against Ferdinand II, Emperor of Austria, and (in 1948) the announcement of a coup d'état by the Communist Party.

The complicated, stratified Old Town Square is now a pedestrian precinct of extremely irregular morphology, lined with a series of mansions, churches, and public buildings erected in different periods but unified by the pastel plastering. The composite City Hall building is set to the west, formed by annexing dwellings to the fourteenth-century main block, so that it appears as a sequence of Gothic and Renaissance buildings, depending on the refurbishments undertaken.

The main block is dominated by a tall tower whose base is decorated by an old astronomical clock with two faces: the upper quadrant tells the time and shows the signs of the zodiac,

26 bottom ■ The square is characterized by the unusual and diversified positioning and morphology of the buildings.

26-27 ■ The view shows the brick façade of the Church of Our Lady Before Týn preceded by the Týn School complex, flanked by the 14th-century "Stone Bell" House.

LOCATION	YEAR OF CONSTRUCTION	AREA	APPLICATION	STYLE
PRAGUE (CZECH REPUBLIC)	14TH CENTURY	APPROXIMATELY 97,000 SQ FEET	RELIGIOUS AND CIVIC SQUARE	STRATIFIED GOTHIC TO ART NOUVEAU

while the lower part is a calendar. As each hour is struck, a mechanism drives a procession composed of the Apostles and several allegorical figures, including Death, the Turk, Vanity and Lust. Opposite, on the east side, there is the 1700s Kinský House, the 1300s "Stone Bell" House, and across the street, the Church of Our Lady Before Týn, also 1300s, whose entrance (via the Týn School) is flanked by another residential building.

The Church of Our Lady Before Týn has a brick façade capped by a pinnacled pediment and decorated with a gold statue of the Virgin Mary, forged from the Utraquist chalice of the Protestant King, Jiri z Podebrad, following defeat of the Hussite reformist nobility who had elected this monarch and for whom the church was the main seat until 1620. In fact, at one corner of the square there is a monument by Ladislav Šaloun dedicated to the religious reformer Jan Hus. It was erected in 1915, on the fifth centennial anniversary of his death at the Council of Konstanz, who had condemned him for heresy. The Kinský House, lavishly decorated with stuccoes and statues, was designed by Kilian Ignaz Dientzenhofer, who also produced the elegant candor of the Church of St. Nicholas, on the opposite side of the square; it was finished in 1735.

Today, the white, Late Baroque mass of St. Nicholas, flanked by two tall belfries and with a cupola frescoed by Kosmas Damian Asam, is the Hussite church, used in summer to host concerts, whilst the Kinský House is used by the National Gallery for art exhibitions. Nearby is the square's most recent building, the Ministry for Social Development, erected in 1898 by Osvald Políkva, using an Art Nouveau style. The south side is characterized by a sequence of porticoed buildings and store windows that preserve the plot's Gothic imprint, whilst the pediments speak of later additions. Here, restaurants, cafes, and galleries lend Staroměstské Náměstí a welcoming air that attracts countless visitors and tourists.

28-29 and 29 top ■ The astronomical clock is part of the city hall's composite construction, and is set in the base of the tall tower that dominates the complex.

29 bottom ■ The bronze monument erected in the square was dedicated to the religious reformer Jan Hus, on the 500th anniversary of his death; it was installed in 1915 by Ladislav Šaloun, and stands out against the backdrop of the Ministry for Social Development, which was built in 1898 by Osvald Políkva.

30 ■ The equestrian statue of Otto von Bismarck, by sculptor Adolf von Hildebrand (1847-1921), inaugurated in 1910, soars above the square.

MARKT

[BREMEN ■ GERMANY]

Markt – literally "market" – is Old Bremen's main square and a fortunate public space, given that the terrible destruction caused by the military bombings in WWII had far less impact on the surrounding buildings. In fact, the *Bremer Rathaus* (city hall) was recently included in the UNESCO World Heritage scheme, to be protected for its unique history and architecture, together with the square itself and the Roland, a majestic 18-feet stat-ue located at its center. The stone Roland, one of Charlemagne's knights, was erected in 1404 to replace a wooden effigy and faces the cathedral. It symbolizes the rights and privileges of the middle classes with respect to those of the church. It is considered the oldest and best-preserved of these types of symbol, which are quite common in medieval German towns.

Markt began to develop in the early fifteenth century, when construction on the cur-

30-31 ■ Aerial view of the Markt space, set between the city hall and the Haus der Bürgerschaft, with the Cathedral of St. Peter visible further back.

rent city hall began in order to replace a twelfth-century edifice. The result divided the area around the Cathedral of St. Peter into two areas, with the cathedral close to the north and the market to the south. The church is set on the highest point and was built in the twelfth century, like the first Rathaus, and oblique to the square, which it faces with a slightly recessed main front. Adjacent to it is the Haus der Bürgerschaft ("citizens' house"), a regional house of parliament with an iron and glass façade. This modernist building was designed by the architect Wassili Luckhard and went up between 1963 to 1966. Opposite it stands the parallelepiped silhouette of the Gothic city hall, renovated from 1595 to 1612 by Lüder von Bentheim, who modernized its features and brought it into the atmosphere of the so-called "Weser Renaissance." In the early 1900s, a neo-Renaissance city hall designed by Gabriel von Seidl was added to the east side.

32-33 ■ Roland, the impressive 18-foot statue of Charlemagne's paladin, symbolizes the rights of the bourgeoisie in Medieval times.

From the sixteenth century on, Markt's south side was occupied by the Schütting, the merchants' corporation premises, which were restored in the 1800s. The nearby *Stadt-waage* or public weighing house was erected in 1588, destroyed during the Second World War, and then rebuilt. The late Renaissance Essinghaus (1618) is also in the vicinity.

Markt has retained an almost rectangular layout over the centuries, and even today it has a slight downward slope. The highest point is the site of the cathedral, whereas the Schütting occupies the lowest point. The paving differs near the most significant buildings and the Roland: a circle divided into sectors outlined by black and white bands, and enclosed by café tables nearby, is delimited by low pilasters. This marks the area defined by the Rathaus, St. Peter, and the Haus der Bürgerschaft.

The old city hall looks out onto Markt, creating a symmetrical order around a central, slightly jutting body, highlighted by a main denticulated tympanum and two side tympanums that emerge against the convex outline of the copper roof. In the brick façade a ground-floor portico is lavishly decorated with stone sculptures, while the double-high sto-

LOCATION	YEAR OF CONSTRUCTION	AREA	APPLICATION	STYLE
BREMEN (GERMANY)	12TH-20TH CENTURY	APPROXIMATELY 26,910 SQ FEET	RELIGIOUS AND CIVIC SQUARE	STRATIFIED ROMANESQUE TO CONTEMPORARY

ry above is lit by enormous windows. The design is echoed by Luckhardt's Haus der Bürgerschaft with a system of ground-floor pilasters that forms an arcade.

This is turn is supported by a curtain wall cadenced by narrow vertical windows that reach to height of the building itself and enclosed by a saw-tooth roof. Initially, the building was unpopular, but it has since become an integral part of the square, just like the Duomo's austere Romanesque façade, which is cut in two by a row of corbels: the lower section featuring four splayed arches, the upper section with a rose window surmounted by a pediment. Two pointed belfries, decorated along their height by a sequence of arched niches that are testimony to the arrival of Gothic influences, flank the façade.

Bremen Markt is more than a historically rich site, it is also a popular location for socializing: even the Rathaus – although located at the rear – has a famous restaurant and wine bar, the renowned Ratskeller ("town council cellar") at whose entrance stands Gerhard Marcks' 1961 statue of Grimm's world-famous Bremen town musicians.

GROTE MARKT

As often occurs with the most iconic squares, Brussels' Grote Markt (Fr. "Grand Place") and its history are closely linked to its location. In 1979, on the occasion of the thousandth anniversary of the founding of Brussels, celebrations inevitably included a revisitation of this great market square's origins and modifications, starting with its name. The oldest written documents that mention the square (then known as the Nedermarckt, or "low market") date back to the mid-twelfth century, but the area had already then been a market for some time.

Initially the area was a swamp, with sandbanks to the south and east, sloping down gently from east to west. This slope is still visible today, and the place names of several dwellings retain the memory of the original terrain as well: number 6 is the Maison Le Cornet, formerly called "La Montagne," number 10 is Maison des Brasseurs, which used to be "de Hille" (from the English *hill*), and number 18 is La Colline or Nouvelle Colline.

34-35 ■ The square's large rectangular space is delineated on the long sides by the 15th-century Hôtel de Ville, characterized by the high central campanile and faced by the neo-Gothic Maison du Roi.

35 right ■ Maison Le Cornet's pediment resembles the stern of a ship and testifies to its having been the ferrymen's corporation premises.

The square's rectangular plan developed over the centuries as the result of the modifications brought by the construction of new private residences and places of trade. Moreover, the municipal authorities intervened several times, to regulate the configuration of the square through demolition and expropriation, so that it was possible to erect more important buildings like the east and west wings of the Hotel de Ville (1401-44), or raise the Beffroi campanile in 1449. The definitive shape was not achieved until the late seventeenth century, after Louis XIV ordered Brussels to be shelled in 1695 as a reprisal for the losses inflicted on the French coastal towns by the English and Dutch warships.

Few of the Grote Markt's buildings survived, but reconstruction was fast and the square acquired the neat harmony that is its distinguishing trait: in 1697, in fact, an edict was issued to define the features required for new buildings. Over time, the Grote Markt has been a theater not only of mercantile and celebratory events but also dramatic ones. It was here, in 1515, that Charles V conferred on Brussels the title of capital of the Low Countries, and it was also here that he signed his abdication in 1555. A few years later the counts Egmont and Hornes were decapitated here, during the Spanish repression led by the Duke of Alba. Later the square hosted the spectacular fireworks display that celebrated the wedding of Maria Theresa of Austria.

LOCATION	YEAR OF CONSTRUCTION	AREA	APPLICATION	STYLE
BRUSSELS (BELGIUM)	12TH-19TH CENTURY	80,500 SQ FEET	MARKET AND CIVIC SQUARE	STRATIFIED GOTHIC TO HISTORICISM

Today the plaza is one of the loveliest in Europe, the linchpin of the capital, the main venue for the city's renowned and colorful flower market and, in the evening, a charming scene whose skillful lighting enhances its features. The two most significant buildings are the Hôtel de Ville and the Maison du Roi, facing one another on the long sides of the Grand Place, isolated by streets whose layout maps out two square blocks: one containing the Hotel de Ville, which occupies most of the south side, and comprises a group of buildings distributed around a rectangular inner court. Its current shape is the result of a reconstruction that followed the 1695 bombing, and in part to 19th-century bombings.

The oldest façade, made up of two tall blocks of three stories surmounted by a steeply sloping roof, with four orders of skylights, dates back to the fifteenth century and looks towards the square where it is built. The main entrance is crowned by the spectacular *Beffroi*, called the *tour inimitable*, over 300 feet in height and terminating in a St. Michael group by Jan van Ruysbroeck (1449). The rear façade, on the other hand, is a 1700s addition, later decorated with statues and pinnacles during restoration. The Maison du Roi owes its name to its patron, the Emperor Charles V, although it was never actually a royal residence: its current layout dates back to a complete reconstruction in 1873, by

P. V. Jamaer, who was inspired by the original and built it in the Gothic style. Today it is a brick building on three floors, a façade featuring arches, a double loggia, a roof with richly-decorated dormer windows, and a central tower with lantern.

All of the houses that look out over the Grote Markt are named for the personal events linked to their building. For instance, the Maison des Boulangers – number 1, on the square's northwest corner, at the junction of Rue au Beurre – is also called Roi d'Espagne because it was decorated with a bust of King Charles II of Spain, erected in 1697, by Jean Cosyn. The Maison de la Louve (number 5) was built in 1691 and is thus named for the relief above the doorway of Romulus and Remus suckled by the she-wolf. Number 6, Maison Le Cornet, presents a tall, narrow façade, with a pediment shaped like a ship's stern, which recalls its having been the premises of the boatmen's corporation. The seven buildings from number 13 to 19, finally, form the Maison Les Ducs de Brabant, unified by a monumental Baroque façade commissioned by the municipal council following the 1695 cannonades. In contrast to this, the façade of Maison Le Cerf, which stands at the corner of Rue de la Colline, is much smaller in size, being only as wide as the distance between the midline of two roof beams. The variety and simultaneous oneness that characterize the Grote Markt led to its being acknowledged, in June 1997, as one of UNESCO's World Heritage sites.

36-37 ■ The square's Christmas decorations are set in front of the Maison du Roi, an elegant building commissioned by Emperor Charles V, but reconstructed in the nineteenth century.

37 ■ The "Beffroi", over 300 feet in height, is topped by the St. Michael group and soars above the Hôtel de Ville entrance, its Christmas illuminations bestowing a particular charm on the whole square.

PIAZZA AND PIAZZETTA
SAN MARCO

[VENICE ■ ITALY]

Piazza San Marco, or St. Mark's Place, is the symbol of Venice worldwide, and a public space dedicated to both civic and religious use that evolved gradually, in parallel with the city around it, as a concrete answer to the demands of a thriving political and religious community. Although it presents coexisting architectural features that range from the Byzantine era to the Renaissance, its current form is mainly attributable to a sixteenth-century intervention that gave it its hallmark: a balanced, harmonious layout opening dramatically onto the Venetian lagoon.

The site was originally chosen as the location for the doge's residence and for the community's first church: San Teodoro or Todaro, dedicated to Theodore, the city's patron saint up to the ninth century, when two Venetian merchants arrived with the remains of St. Mark the Evangelist. In the eleventh century the piazza still had not acquired the size it has now: it was at that time crossed at about a third of the way from where the basilica stands by the Batario Canal, and beyond that the San Zaccaria convent garden and the church of San Geminiano. Historical reconstruction suggests that opposite the ducal palace, towards the lagoon, no smaller square or *piazzetta* existed: the water formed a moat, as it were, that reached as far as the basilica foundations, where a canal apparently ran, leaving the

38 ■ Gentile Bellini, 16th-century painter, depicted the procession in St. Mark's Square: the painting shows, on the right, the buildings that existed before Vincenzo Scamozzi's intervention, which led to the construction of the Procuratie Nuove.

39 ■ The campanile, which collapsed in 1902, was rebuilt by Luca Beltrami and Gaetano Moretti "exactly how and where it was", in a solitary corner position between St. Mark's Square and Piazzetta San Marco. The basilica and the Doge's Palace stand out in the background, reflected in the high tide.

40 top ■ The astronomical clock adorns the Torre dell'Orologio, started in 1496.

40 bottom ■ With our backs to the basilica, the square appears as a large trapezium, closed off to the right by the Procuratie Vecchie, the closing side finished by Jacopo Sansovino, and, on the left, by the Procuratie Nuove, the work of Vincenzo Scamozzi.

building totally surrounded by water. Today's square, which runs 570 feet (175.5 meters) from the basilica façade, is therefore the result of complex and composite urban transformations – and a density of historical events and traditions in a relatively concentrated space.

In the mid-twelfth century, when the city was governed by Doge Sebastiano Ziani, the Batario Canal was interred, and the square doubled in length by acquiring the convent garden and demolishing and relocating the church of San Geminiano; further, the *piazzetta* was created by filling in the moat and the canals around the doge's home. From the thirteenth to the fifteenth century, the basilica's exterior layout was completed, shaping the "onion" cupolas and covering the façade with slabs of marble, sculptures, mosaics, and mock Gothic lancet arches. Similarly interventions were made at the doge's

40-41 ▪ The aerial view shows the square's floor plan: a trapezium that opens onto
the lagoon across the piazzetta space, also a trapezium, but on a much smaller scale.
All the bulk of the buildings lining the sides of both spaces are evident.

LOCATION	YEAR OF CONSTRUCTION	AREA	APPLICATION	STYLE
VENICE (ITALY)	12TH-19TH CENTURY	14,200 SQ FEET 38,879 SQ FEET	RELIGIOUS AND CIVIC SQUARE	STRATIFIED BYZANTINE TO RENAISSANCE

palace, whose interior was renovated to meet the changing needs of the city's political-ad-
ministrative structure; in 1422 work began on the façade looking out toward the Piazzetta,
which acquired the appearance it still has today.

Next came Torre dell'Orologio, the clock tower begun in 1496, possibly designed by Mau-
ro Codussi, and in 1514 the rebuilding of the Procuratie Vecchie, the residences of the
Procuratori di San Marco, the highest-ranking officials after the doge, began, resulting in
the current row of buildings, which completed and unified the square's northern face. The
definitive intervention on the layout took place in the 1500s, however, when Jacopo Sansovino completed the section of the Procuratie Vecchie that defines the short side opposite
St. Mark's. Sansovino designed the new façade for the church of San Geminiano, where the
Procuratie finished, and rebuilt the loggetta at the base of the Campanile and the Zecca.
Lastly he dealt with the Libreria Marciana, the kingpin of the new urban layout that was
later to include Vincenzo Scamozzi's Procuratie Nuove.

42-43 ■ **Two columns leading into the Piazzetta hold the symbols of the city: St. Mark's Lion and the statue of St. Theodore.**

The last transformations occurred in the 1700s, when the piazza was repaved in trachyte by Andrea Tirali, and in the early 1800s when the San Geminiano church was demolished and replaced by a section completing the Procuratie Nuove, called the Napoleonic Wing, while towards the lagoon, the granaries at Terranova were razed.

Nowadays the piazza is a large trapezoidal space with its long side facing the curving silhouette of St. Mark's, which is its backdrop. The campanile, rebuilt in 1902, is detached from the main construction, acting as a pivot in the transition from the large square to the piazzetta, another trapezoidal space set against a scenario that has the clock tower on one side and the lagoon on the other.

The Libreria Marciana, with the cadenced iteration of its ground floor colonnade arches, serves as the hinging element between the two squares, facing onto the piazzetta but turned towards St. Mark's Square, and confirming its function as a civic forum. The Libreria is a Renaissance creation, with departures from Mannerism: aside from the system of arches supported by pillars and semi-columns holding up the ground-floor architrave, the upper story introduces split balusters and contracted serlianas ending in the richly-ornamented frieze.

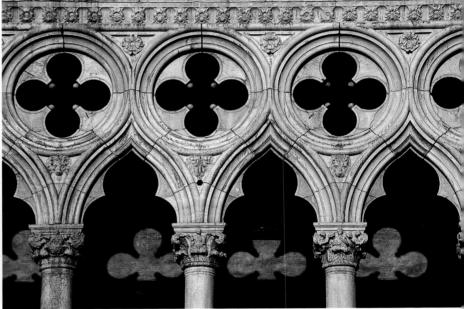

The Procuratie Nuove continue toward St. Mark's Square from the extremity of the Libreria Marciana, aligned with it and raised a storey higher. In 1810, thanks to work by Giuseppe Soli, they were joined to the Procuratie Vecchie, which were also colonnaded, with an extension of seven bays and concealment of the height difference achieved with an attic decorated with sculptures. The arcade system thus united the three prospects of St. Mark's Square, returning in the Piazzetta, in the Libreria's Renaissance order and in the late Gothic Palazzo Ducale, arranged on lancet arches and historiated capitals that support a loggia with inflected arches. The façade, finished with geometric cross patterns of red, white and gray marble, has a mock Byzantine coping turned at right angles to the pier.

Sansovino's Zecca, a mint which has housed part of the library since 1905, and the gardens that replaced the demolished Terranova granaries, are on the opposite side, beyond the Libreria colonnade. Two monolithic columns open the way from the lagoon to the small square: one holds the Lion of St. Mark and the other a statue of St. Theodore, the city's first patron saint.

43 top ■ The red porphyry sculpture group depicts the Tetrarchs: Diocletian, Galerius, Maximilian and Costantius. The opus, situated on the corner of the basilica nearest the Doge's Palace, was brought from Constantinople, and dates back to the 3rd-4th century.

43 bottom ■ A sequence of lancet arches and the lavish Late Gothic ornamentation of the Doge's Palace greet visitors arriving from the lagoon.

PIAZZA DEL
CAMPIDOGLIO

[ROME ■ ITALY]

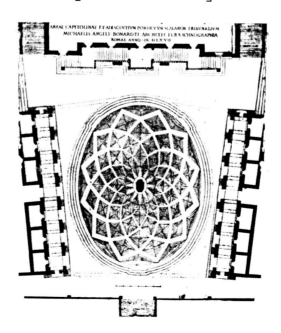

44-45 ■ Michelangelo's Piazza del Campidoglio, masterpiece of Renaissance architecture, is the backdrop to the Fori Imperiali. The trapezoidal square enclosed by Palazzo Senatorio, flanked by Palazzo dei Conservatori and Palazzo Nuovo. The Ara Coeli is visible on the left.

44 bottom ■ Bartolomeo Faleti published Piazza del Campidoglio's layout as designed by Michelangelo: the orientation function of the central ellipsis, which underscores the pathway from the staircase to Palazzo Senatorio, and the famous star-shaped paving outline, are evident.

Piazza del Campidoglio, or Capitol Square, is a worldwide icon of Italian Renaissance architecture designed by Michelangelo following a series of measures taken by Pope Paul III. The square has become the symbol of an era characterized by marvelous urban renovation schemes. The piazza sits on Capitoline Hill, which was originally two peaks separated by a col, the "Capitolium" and the "Arx." The hill was a prime location for temples and public buildings, and soon became the fulcrum of religious and civil life in ancient Rome, dominating the Forum valley and the plain of Campo Marzio.

In A.D. 78 the dip between the two peaks was covered by the construction of the Tabularium, an archive for laws and treaties which is now the underpinning to the Senate Palace in the square created by Michelangelo. The hill was later abandoned, except for the construction of Santa Maria in Ara Coeli, in the ninth or tenth century, and the Corsi family palazzo, which was later occupied by the Senate in the twelfth century – a symbol of the birth of a new commune free of the papal yoke. Another building, the Palazzo dei Conservatori, was erected next to this palazzo at the time of Michelangelo's new designs and was occupied by the Capitoline Chamber, Rome's civic administration.

In 1538, when Paul III decided to move the statue thought to be Marcus Aurelius (from St. John Lateran to the Capitol (it is now in the Capitoline Museum), Michelangelo found himself intervening in an unwieldy situation with scant financial means. Other works were added – Castor and Pollux, Constantine and his son Constant, two milliary columns with

inscriptions by Nerva and Vespasian – in the aim to concentrate works in the city's ideal center, a place always considered the seat and symbol of the greatness of ancient Rome. Michelangelo succeeded in giving a concrete form to this intention, using Marcus Aurelius as a visual kingpin for the composition, and establishing the statue at the center of the trapezoidal square he had designed. The plan cleverly derives from the disorganized juxtaposition of the two existing buildings.

Since the Senate Palace, installed as a backdrop to the square, and Palazzo dei Conservatori are set at an 80° angle to one another, the architect conceived a second building, Palazzo Nuovo, with the same angulation as the first, in order to achieve a geometrically consistent layout. The shorter side of the trapezium, facing the city, is protected by a baluster decorated with Roman statues and broken by an access staircase that covers the entire length of the hill slope, flanked by the Ara Coeli ramp. The long side, on the other hand, lines up towards the Senate Palace to create a perspective arena that adapts to the existing roads and opens as two points onto the Roman Forum behind it, finding a precedent in Bernardo Rossellino's refurbishment of Pienza's town square.

Thanks to the organization of the existing access roads – two coming from the Forum and two in front of the baluster and monumental staircase – and thanks to the paving, Michelangelo managed to coordinate the various buildings, intervening on principles of axiality, symmetry, and convergence. In fact, the floor ellipse perfectly combines the central space with the presence of a main axis facing the main building, Palazzo dei Conservatori, thereby directing a visitor's visual perception.

46 and 46-47 ■ The Dioscuri, the mythological Castor and
Pollux, were positioned at the entrance to the square
in the 16th century, after Paul III, who commissioned
the refurbishment of the Capitoline Hill, ordered that
the effigy of Marcus Aurelius be transferred to the
centre of the square, with subsequent repositioning
of numerous other groups of statues.

LOCATION	YEAR OF CONSTRUCTION	AREA	APPLICATION	STYLE
ROME (ITALY)	16TH-17TH CENTURY	APPROXIMATELY 32,300 SQ FEET	CIVIC SQUARE	RENAISSANCE

The square is set slightly lower than the level of the buildings, which is sufficient to underscore the

five separate entrances, but towards the center it rises slightly to their level. The dynamic star pattern was created in 1940 by Antonio Muñoz, based on a 1567 etching, and enhances the central position of the Marcus Aurelius statue. These elements indicate that the classical harmony of the early Renaissance had already been discarded, influencing development of subsequent architecture. The entire complex was subjected to long and meticulous restorations in the 1990s.

The composition of the square is not perceivable from below since it was conceived as a large open space enclosed by three walls. It can be seen from above by ascending the steps and standing in the square to capture its solemnity. Michelangelo may only have modified the façades of the two existing buildings, but his interven-

48-49 ■ The equestrian monument, probably of Marcus Aurelius, is set in front of Palazzo Senatorio, at the center of the star-shaped paving.

tion succeeded in endowing them with depth and architectural and planning character.
In fact, he introduced a double staircase on the front of Palazzo dei Conservatori, leading directly to the first floor, to create a visual balance with the first order of the other two buildings.

The ground floor, originally used as a prison, became a base on which the giant order
of Corinthian pilaster strips is arranged, separating the upper part of the façade into
seven bays. Rectangular windows with alternating curved and triangular tympana are installed in each bay, and the sequence is broken only by the entrance. This sequence, but
using only curved tympana, was recovered in Palazzo dei Conservatori, and continues on
the side head of the building with a ground floor arcade. The giant order of Corinthian
pilaster strips acts as vertical unification of the façade, overlapping the portico pilasters and flanked by the two columns on which the piano nobile floor architrave rests.
Palazzo Nuovo, built after Michelangelo's death by Girolamo and Carlo Rainaldi, uses a similar criterion taken from the artist's original plan.

KRASNAJA
PLOŠČAD'

[MOSCOW ■ RUSSIA]

50-51 ■ The colored cupolas
of the famous St. Basil
Cathedral conceal the
Red Square's vast area,
destination of numerous
tourists and visitors.

To the mind's eye Krasnaja ploščad' (Red Square) is the quintessence of Russia itself. Even its name is fraught with meaning, for the ancient term "krasnaja" does not translate as "red" but "beautiful" or "best," so the square is "beautiful" by sheer definition. This name, in any case, is relatively recent: the first written references to the area date back to a fifteenth-century chronicle in which it is described as a market. Later, in the sixteenth century, it was called Troickaja – "the Trinity" – from the name of the church located there. After the terrible fire of 1571, it became the "square of the fire," whereas the current name was used only from the seventeenth century on.

The history and the actual origins of the square are linked indissolubly to the Kremlin, whose walls close one side. In the late fifteenth century, after the new walls were built, Ivan III forbade, for defensive reasons, any constructions in the area to the east of the fortified citadel; the reason being that this side, unlike the others, did not enjoy the protection afforded by water. With the elimina-

tion of the small dwellings that had existed there up to that point, a huge square emerged where trade could be plied only by street vendors who would not obscure the view. From now on, surprise attacks by enemies were made nigh impossible. As time passed the prohibition was set aside, and in the so-called "plan of Peter," an architectural blueprint of sorts found in Peter the Great's Chancellery and made known abroad as early as 1597 – there is an illustration of how the square appeared in the late sixteenth century. The walls are bordered by moats with bridges crossing them, and the square, which was then far larger than it is now, is dotted with numerous shops sloping down to the Moskva.

The sketch also shows St. Basil's Cathedral, a round stone platform called Lobnoe Mesto, set to the east of the cathedral, the small church of St. Nicholas on the Moskva, four rows of shops, the marketplace, and two isbas where the History Museum now stands. The oldest surviving structures on the square are thus the Kremlin complex (fifteenth-sixteenth century), St. Basil's Cathedral (sixteenth century) and the Lobnoe Mesto (sixteenth century), the latter used not only for capital punishments but also for proclaiming heirs to the throne. Following Napoleon's retreat, the shops were removed for good and, in 1818, Moscow's first civil monument was inaugurated to celebrate the rebirth of the city.

50 bottom ■ The bronze monument dedicated to Kozma Minin and Dimitri Pozarskij, realized in 1818, is set at the south of the square, between Lobnoe Mesto and St. Basil's Cathedral.

52-53 ■ The multiform profile of St. Basil's Cathedral, with its nine onion-shaped cupolas, closes off one end of the Red Square's vast rectangular area.

A civil monument to Minin and Pozarskij was realized by public subscription and placed at the south
of the square, between Lobnoe Mesto and St. Basil's
Cathedral.

As the 1800s drew to a close, another two significant projects were completed: the construction
(1878-83) of the History Museum to a design by the
English architect, Vladimir Sherwood, and, shortly after that, a commercial building comprising three orders of arcades with glass and iron framework
roofing, an opus by Aleksandr Pomerancev (1888-93)
and the forerunner of today's famed GUM department store.

In 1929-30, a few years after Lenin's death, a red
granite mausoleum designed by Aleksej Ščusec (with a
sarcophagus by Konstantin Melnikov) was erected to
house his remains,. Thus the modern-day plaza is dominated to the east by Lenin's massive tomb comprised
of a square-based, truncated and terraced pyramid,
and surmounted by a colonnade (also granite).

54 bottom ■ The
Voskressensky Gate
opens onto Red Square,
with two arched portals
surmounted by two twin
towers topped by tall
pinnacles.

LOCATION	YEAR OF CONSTRUCTION	AREA	APPLICATION	STYLE
MOSCOW (RUSSIA)	12TH-20TH CENTURY	APPROXIMATELY 248,000 SQ FEET	RELIGIOUS AND CIVIC SQUARE	STRATIFIED RENAISSANCE TO SOCIALIST REALISM

The Kremlin ("fortified citadel") is opposite, to the west, and incarnates the expression of power embraced by its crenellated battlements with swallowtails that are a clear declaration of the approach chosen by the Sforza architects, Antonio Solari and Marco Ruffo, who were commissioned by Tsar Ivan III ("the Great"), together with other Italian artists. The walls around the square are cadenced by six defensive towers, and behind them stand the Arsenal, the Senate, and the Soviet Palace. The History Museum, a large historicist building resounding with the Russian decorative tradition, closes the north side and is home to the testimonies of the populations that inhabited Russia from prehistory to the modern age. Lastly, to the south, there is the curving profile of St. Basil's Cathedral, commissioned by Tsar Ivan IV ("the Terrible") after his victory over the Tartars and the conquest of Kazan. Famous for its brightly-colored cupolas, whose bulbular onion-like forms cap the nine chapels that make up the cathedral, St. Basil's is not only the icon of the square, but also of the entire city of Moscow.

54-55 ■ The spectacular cathedral of St. Basil soars breathtaking against the horizontal profile of the Kremlin's fortified walls, cadenced by solid towers.

SULTANAHMET
MEIDANI

[ISTANBUL ■ TURKEY]

Istanbul, Turkey's biggest city, overlooking the gleaming scenario of the Bosporus, where East meets West, bridges two different cultural universes. This aspect is clearly illustrated by the ancient origins of today's Sultan Ahmet Square, known locally as Sultanahmet Meidani, the garden-square separating St. Sophia and the Blue Mosque. In the Roman period it was actually the site of the Augusteion, the forum of Augustus and, the kingpin of the entire urban extension that irradiated from it. The celebrated basilica of St. Sophia (or Aya

56-57 ■ This aerial view shows the gardens of the square, set between the magnificent Blue Mosque and St. Sophia, with the Hammam of Roxelana next to it.

Sofya) was built by order of the Emperor Justinian, from 532 to 537, and even now demarcates the north side of the square, whereas the imperial palace, the patriarchate and the senate, ordered by Constantine the Great, have all been lost. The great spa of Zeuxippus, once located south of the ancient forum, has also gone, replaced by the splendid Sultanahmet Cami, known in English as the Blue Mosque because of the color that dominates dominates the decorative scheme of its lavish interior decorative scheme.

The Blue Mosque was built by Mehemet Agha, a pupil of Sinan, the most important architect in the Turkish Classical period, who in 1556 also worked for Suleiman the Magnificent to build the so-called "Hammam of Roxelana", Turkish baths that occupy the northeast side of the square. The Mosque is a later building, however, erected from 1609 to 1616, using plans drawn up by Sinan. It was part of a huge complex that included services like a bazaar, a hospital, schools, public kitchens and a mausoleum for Sultan Ahmet.

LOCATION	YEAR OF CONSTRUCTION	AREA	APPLICATION	STYLE
ISTANBUL (TURKEY)	6TH-17TH CENTURY	APPROXIMATELY 65,000 SQ FEET	RELIGIOUS AND CIVIC SQUARE	STRATIFIED BYZANTINE TO LOCAL CLASSICAL PERIOD

Few of these structures have survived, just as few traces remain of the Roman period, extending along the south-east side of the mosque and the square: these are the ruins of the Hippodrome of Byzantium, which that was built by order of Septimius Severus and which occupied a huge area during the reign of Constantine the Great.

The space between St. Sophia, now a museum, the Blue Mosque, and the Hammam of Roxelana, which is converted into now a showroom and sales outlet for Turkish carpets and kilims, is a large, square garden. It is split into two quadrants around a circular basin of water and is typically decked with flowerbeds and lavish Mediterranean trees and plants, denser near the basilica and the Turkish baths, whose small, elegant cupolas emerge from amidst the tree fronds. The powerful, airy mass of Aya Sofya's cupola, on the other hand, looms majestic over the entire garden, flanked by four robust minarets added in 1453, following the Turkish victory over Rome, and the building's its subsequent conversion from cathedral to to a mosque. Viewing its majestic dome, Seeing it soar towhich soars above dominate its surroundings and dominates the entire skyline, it is easy to understand why it stands with the Parthenon and the Pantheon as a treasured symbol of ancient Western architecture.

58-59 ■ The square opens
in a sequence of green-
framed flowerbeds and
fountains, against the
backdrop of the Blue
Mosque and the Bosporus.

59 top ■ The massive
cupola of the famous
basilica of St. Sophia
is the backdrop to
the luxuriant vegetation
and neat flowerbeds
of this garden square.

59 bottom ■ The Blue Mosque closes one side
of Sultanahmet Meidani, with its distinctive
silhouette of six minarets and sequence
of cupolas and semi-cupolas.

Today's square is actually often called Aya Sofya Meidani, although the official name is Sultanahmet Meidani. The basilica-museum is, in fact, directly connected to the garden-square, traced with pedestrian pathways that unite it with the main traffic thorough-fare, which in turn separates it from the Blue Mosque, framed by its own sequence of flowerbeds. So it is the silhouette of Sultan Ahmet Cami, which that elegantly seals off the green space, with its resolute sequence of cupolas and semi cupolas of various sizes; these, resting amidst six slender minarets that define the outer perimeter. It is the only mosque in Istanbul to have been built with as many as six minarets and is certainly a fine counterpoint to the powerful bulk of St. Sophia. Tourists strolling here today will not fail to be impressed by the monumental scale of the buildings.

PIAZZA
NAVONA

[ROME ▪ ITALY]

Piazza Navona, a Baroque icon that stands second only to the capital's more famous St. Peter's Square, is the noteworthy result of centuries of layered urban schemes. It was standardized to its current layout by a seventeenth-century intervention. The name of the piazza ("big ship") is commonly attributed to its elongated boat shape, with the differing extremities – one slightly oblique, the other semicircular, like a ship's stern – and also because in the past it was flooded twice a year: in August, to allow the papal court to parade its boats, and at carnival, for the nobility to do likewise in their carriages. The custom of flooding the square in summer was initiated to dampen the heat and continued until the nineteenth century, although there were interruptions during epidemics. It was definitively prohibited in 1865.

The square stands where Domitian built his stadium, which was inaugurated in A.D. 86 to celebrate the Capitoline Agon. The stadium could hold 30,000 spectators and was laid out exactly as today's square. The area has never been abandoned, an example and confirmation of the law of the "permanence of layout," where the conditioning of the form and the repeated use of existing foundations ensures that topographical characteristics are handed down from a historical condition to the present day. In the eighth century the stadium hosted several oratorios and, subsequently, the monastery and church of Sant' Agnese, the parish church of San Nicola and, later, San Giacomo.

In about the thirteenth century, houses and towers were built, and the area gradually became the center of urban life in the Tiber loop.

60 ▪ Preparations for celebrations in Piazza Navona are shown against the backdrop of Francesco Borromini's church of Sant'Agnese in Agone and gathered around Gian Lorenzo Bernini's Fountain of the Rivers, surmounted by an obelisk.

61 ▪ Piazza Navona's famous bowl unfolding in its elegant greatness.

62-63 ■ Gian Lorenzo Bernini's Fountain of the Rivers, erected in 1651, was the sculptor's work that won Pope Innocent X's favor. Set in the center of the square, it is surmounted by an obelisk brought from the Circus of Maxentius.

In 1477 the market previously held at the Capitol was moved here, where it stayed until 1869, when it was transferred to Campo dei Fiori. Proof that the area was significant in urban life comes from Giuliano da Sangallo's project for connecting the piazza via a series of arcades to Palazzo Medici (now Palazzo Madama), which the architect was building at that time. In the fifteenth century there were still terraces that, up to that time, had conditioned the installation of buildings towards exterior of the cavea and allowed people to watch the military drills conducted there.

The pope responsible for the modifications that transformed the square into what it is today – one of the world's most admired Baroque masterpieces – was Innocent X, a member of the Pamphili family. He decided to turn the piazza where his family residence stood into a symbol of Roman magnificence, and he went as far as taxing the owners of buildings that faced the square so that in 1646 he was able to initiate his program of demolitions, alignments, and general reorganization, all of which redefined the configuration.

63 ■ Admirable personifications of the Nile, Ganges, Danube and Rio de la Plata, by different sculptors, are installed around the fountain.

64-65 and 65 ■ The Moro fountain is on the south side of the square, aligned with the other fountains along its central axis. The name derives from the statue of the Ethiopian (Moor) battling with the dolphin, made to a design by Bernini, while the multilobed basin is by Giacomo Della Porta; the bowl in which it is placed was designed by Borromini.

Innocent X requested contributions from numerous architects: Gian Lorenzo Bernini, for the Fountain of the Four Rivers; Francesco Borromini, who alternated with Girolamo and Carlo Rainaldi both for the renovation of the Pope's ancestral home and for the new church of Sant'Agnese in Agone. It was thanks to the installation of the three fountains and related plumbing, in 1652, that lake entertainment could be transferred here: by closing the fountain drainage pipes, water flooded the square so it could be used for the events illustrated in so many prints and etchings of the period.

In the centuries that followed, except for some limited modifications to several of the great palazzi located there, the layout of the square did not change, and in the nineteenth century a scheme to replace the 1485 paving with a garden was rejected, while in 1936, notwithstanding lavish designs by Marcello Piacentini for the semicircular side of the square, the derelict buildings located there were rebuilt to exactly the same style. At this moment in time, therefore, Piazza Navona's large bowl is delimited by almost uninterrupted curtains of buildings. To the west stands the Palazzo Pamphili sequence and Sant'Agnese,

LOCATION	YEAR OF CONSTRUCTION	AREA	APPLICATION	STYLE
ROME (ITALY)	17TH CENTURY	APPROXIMATELY 124,00 SQ FEET	RELIGIOUS AND CIVIC SQUARE	BAROQUE

followed by two groups of dwellings broken by the entrance to Via Santa Maria dell'Anima; to the east, the built-up section opens in just one point, towards Corso del Rinascimento; to the north, the curved side is connected to Piazza Cinque Lune, whereas to the south four streets enter the oblique side, isolating Palazzo Braschi there. Three fountains plot out the lengthwise axis of the piazza, drawing attention to the central piece designed by Bernini, which is dominated by the obelisk rising from the free-form rock base and supported by personifications of the rivers Nile, Ganges, Danube, and Rio de la Plata. The earlier Moor fountain is set to the south, enhanced in 1654 by the statue of an Ethiopian battling with a dolphin, and to the north is the Neptune fountain, whose sculpture was not added until 1878, to create symmetry with the Moor piece.

The overwhelming masterpiece of the piazza is nonetheless Sant'Agnese in Agone, with its understated concave façade enclosed by two belfries that draw the eye to the cupola and conceal the church's central Greek cross floorplan. According to Borromini's design (though it was completed by Carlo Rainaldi) the church was connected to neighboring Palazzo Pamphili and the Collegio di Sant'Agnese, thus contributing to the overall idea of a coherent and unitary image for the square.

ST. PETER'S
SQUARE

[THE VATICAN]

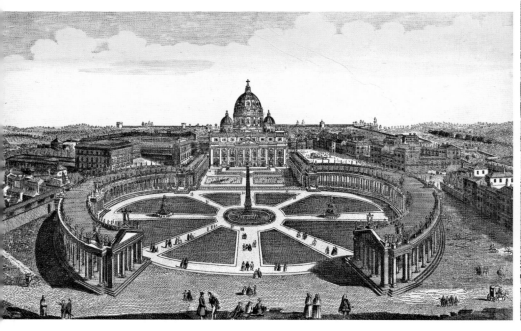

The huge ellipse of St. Peter's Square, designed by Bernini for Pope Alexander VII, is 780 feet (240 meters) wide, or 858 feet (264 meters) if measured from the façade to the portico alignment on the axis. For all intents and purposes it is an unparalleled masterpiece, both for its architecture and the scenario. With the lengthening of St. Peter's nave and the building of the façade by Carlo Maderno, a series of proposals for refurbishing the square were put forward by Maderno himself, and by Ferrabosco, Bartoli Spada, Rainaldi, not to mention the sculptor and architect Gian Lorenzo Bernini.

Bernini's plans prevailed over all others and were successful in creating a harmonious link with the church, making it the backdrop to the square, as opposed to the idea of Michelangelo and Bramante before him, both of whom had perceived it as separate. For many years the popes had been concerned with refurbishing the area in front of the church: in 1586, Pope Sixtus V moved the obelisk from the side of the basilica to its current position, and in 1656 this became the center of the new square, between the two ex-

66 ■ **The French printer Hocquart depicted the function of Gian Lorenzo Bernini's Colonnade, welcoming the devout as they arrived at St. Peter's, and accentuating the basilica's symmetrical construction.**

tremities of the ellipse occupied by magnificent fountains. Since the obelisk and one of fountains were installed before Bernini's intervention, they were constraints and, equally, stimuli for the clever solution invented by the architect.

Papal intention was to transform the square into a space that was closely connected to and useful for the religious building, which is a preeminent symbol of Christianity. Bernini himself interpreted these intentions in his work and in his own words, declaring he had completed the piazza so it would open its arms like a mother to Catholics, to confirm their belief; to heretics, to embrace them into the Church; and to infidels, to light the way to true faith. The seventeenth-century innovations were therefore threefold: the lengthened church, the "enclosed" piazza (St. Peter's Square), and the "open" square, known as Piazza Rusticucci.

Bernini's original idea included a third arcaded element interposed between the two colonnade wings that have gone down in history.

66-67 ■ **Looking out from the basilica, we will observe the pincer basin that extends into the Bernini colonnades, and the axial layout that stretches into Via della Conciliazione, opened by Marcello Piacentini between 1937 and 1950, demolishing the historical quarter called "spina dei borghi".**

LOCATION	YEAR OF CONSTRUCTION	AREA	APPLICATION	STYLE
ROME (VATICAN CITY)	1656-1667	APPROXIMATELY 371,350 SQ FEET	RELIGIOUS SQUARE	BAROQUE

The only remaining trace of the third structure can be found in etchings and floor plans of the period, and some early photographs hand down a suggestion of Piazza Rusticucci, which no longer exists, demolished alongside the entire Borgo quarter, as required by Marcello Piacentini's scheme to open up Via della Conciliazione, from 1937 to 1950. Nonetheless, for three centuries, the two squares coexisted, the latter contributing to enhance the view of the former (Bernini's masterpiece) and accentuating the visual effect of Michelangelo's cupola, which was given its final boost by the new twentieth-century avenue.

The piazza is defined by the sequence of two spaces that valorize the basilica. The first has a trapezoidal plan, modeled on the Pienza and Campidoglio squares, and is the location of the parvis, with two wings that start from the actual church, gradually closing in as they proceed, then open up into the second basin, which comprises a magnificent, convivial ellipse that welcomes the devout. The two "corridors" that border the trapezium in front of the religious building are closed on the outside, penetrated by windows, and have

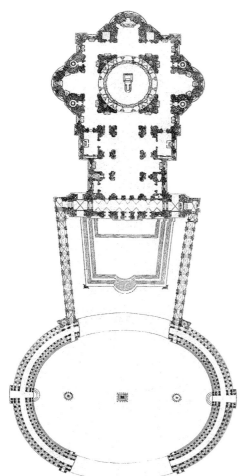

68-69 ■ The view shows the majestic complex of St. Peter's basilica in relation to the monumental layout of the square.

69 bottom ■ The floor plan shows Michelangelo's original layout, with the extension introduced by Carlo Maderno and the "corridors" conceived by Gian Lorenzo Bernini.

pilaster strips that cadence the approach of believers to the basilica. Where the corridors end, the basilica portico begins, and on the right takes to the vestibule with its "Scala Regia" staircase, another of Bernini's masterpieces, leading into the Vatican buildings.

Four series of impressive travertine Tuscanic columns make up the two pincer hemicycles that outline the piazza, creating three paths, of which the largest is in the center. If observed from a specific standpoint, not far from the

fountains and marked on the paving, the four rows of columns seem to merge into one and create a striking optical illusion: the colonnade, in point of fact, comprises 284 elements, raised by three steps above the level of the square.

The corridors and the colonnade are kept at the same height so that St. Peter's, and the Vatican buildings behind it, can be seen in the distance. Their composition is unified by the continuity of the plain tripartite architrave that completes them and is a clear reference to the trilithic system used in Greek architecture. Moreover, the architrave supports a baluster decorated with countless statues, each installed near a column or pilaster strip beneath; lastly, the two hemicycles end in a gable where they reach the city. The porphyry cube paving is divided by natural stone elements that form curving trapezoidal sectors converging towards the center, with its obelisk, and opened to align with the colonnade.

The ellipse's main axis cuts transversally across the church's lengthwise axis and aligns the obelisk and the two fountains, which are the focal points. This dual focus, in other words the presence of two centers, is at one and the same time an expression of centrality and dynamism, characteristics of the scenographic Baroque research that the Roman architect designed – and executed – to perfection.

70-71 ■ From the basilica
facade, Michelangelo's cupola,
designed with a ribbed dome
and oculi, soars solemnly,
its destiny to watch over
the religious celebrations
that are a regular
occurrence in the square.

71 top ■ A statue of St. Peter
symbolically grasps the key
that opens the gates to
the Kingdom of Heaven.

71 bottom ■ Numerous
marble statue groups
finish the terminals of the
colonnades and the wings: the
papal bearings are included.

PLACE DES
VOSGES

[PARIS ■ FRANCE]

Formerly Place Royale, Place des Vosges is one of three squares commissioned by Henry IV after he became king. His intention was to transform Paris, then still rooted in the Middle Ages, into a city that would feel and experience – like Florence, Rome, and Venice – the ferment and innovation of a Renaissance already mature in Italy. Combined with the stimuli of a new artistic era, he hoped this would to lead France into the modern age. Henry IV had inherited a very difficult situation: the Hundred Years War and religious wars were not yet completely resolved and had impeded urban renewal of the capital, which had been in English hands until 1436, weakening royal power. Henry IV's action began a full-scale recovery of France, and Paris's transformation came about thanks to an intensive urban-planning and restyling program that symbolized the rebirth of central power. It heralded the establishment of the monarchy, which was later reinforced to the point of being represented by a figure like Louis XIV.

Work to build Place Royale / Place des Vosges (as it was rechristened by Napoleon) began in 1605, but by 1604, the square had already been conceived and initiated by the sovereign, proved unequivocally by his letter patent defining the parameters for completion of the works. If there is now no doubt that the piazza (town square) was invented by the Italians, in all likelihood it began to take on a specific morphology and typology in France, from the seventeenth to the eighteenth century. The squares commissioned by Henry IV: Place Royale, Place Dauphine (begun in 1607) and Place de France (conceived in 1608), are different

 72-73 ■ The aerial view shows the square's regular geometry, with pedestrian paths separated by flowerbeds, the plan adjusting to the architectural continuity of the buildings that cadence the perimeter.

LOCATION	YEAR OF CONSTRUCTION	AREA	APPLICATION	STYLE
PARIS (FRANCE)	1604-1612	APPROXIMATELY 204,500 SQ FEET	CIVIC SQUARE	BAROQUE

but share some features: they are geometrical in layout, respectively square, triangular and semicircular; their names are chosen to glorify the king, his family, or the kingdom; lastly, the function was no longer monumental or with civic scope, as was the case in Italy. In the first two cases, it was commercial, and aimed at the bourgeoisie; in the latter it was administrative. Henry IV never saw the three squares completed. He died prematurely in 1610, assassinated by a fanatic who considered him a Huguenot, too close to the old coreligionists.

Victor Hugo, who lived in Place des Vosges, wrote that the square owed its origins to a spear blow; and it was, in fact, a lance that killed Henry II, after piercing his eye. His widow, Catherine de' Medici, persuaded her son, Charles IX, to allow her to demolish the Hôtel des Tournelles, one of the four royal residences in the capital, where Henry had died after ten days of agony. The large area that became available was used initially as a horse market, until Henry IV decided it should become a commercial site where businesses could be set up to foster the capital's economic revival. In an effort to restart the economy, after many years of civil war, it was decided to concentrate on the textile sector, especially silk, to become independent of Italian imports. Consequently, a silk factory was built to the north, on one side of the square, and the other sides were used to build homes for the workers.

The enterprise failed to achieve the results that had been expected, and the square soon changed its function and became the heart of high-society life. In fact, as early as April 1612, it

74-75 ■ The four harmonious, tree-lined sides of Place des Vosges appear in their elegant unity, thanks to the sequence of buildings that uniformly curtain all sides the perimeter.

75 ■ A fountain is installed in each corner of this garden square.

was of the venue for the wedding of Louis XIII and Anne of Austria. In 1639 a statue of Louis XIII on horseback was erected in the centre of the square (though destroyed during the French Revolution, it was replaced in 1821). The success of this new type of plaza, with an equestrian statue of the king (in this case Louis XIII) in its center, spread to many European cities, and was especially popular in England, where the expression "*place royale*" was used to indicate this specific genre.

The square has retained its original rectangular layout and is still closed, like a cloister, by buildings with three orders that feature a colonnaded ground floorholding luxury stores, galleries, and restaurants. Place des Vosges is thus an excellent example of seventeenth-century Paris, having retained that era's organization and characteristics over the centuries. The curtain of constructions comprises thirty-six symmetrical buildings designed for the bourgeoisie, a fact that can be surmised from the size of the accommodations. The layout of the buildings is further valorized by the presence, at the center of each of the two opposite sides, of the *Pavillon du Roi* and the *Pavillon de la Reine*, which are one storey higher than the other structures. The *Pavillon du Roi* is easy to recognize, since it stands out for its lavish splendor. The architecture is in late French Renaissance style, the chronological equivalent of Italian Baroque, and was an early prelude to the establishment over the new Classicism that became evident in Claude Perrault's construction of the eastern façade of the Louvre, in the late 1600s.

Even today, the red brick and white stone buildings of this grand square, with their two orders of windows set up above the colonnaded arches and the tall dormer windows under the slate roofs, express the sort of charm that convinces visitors they really are in Paris. Nor does it hurt that almost all of the square's pedestrian area is now planted with a tree-lined bank and flowerbeds – a finishing touch to the atmosphere of this truly memorable site.

PLACE
VENDÔME

[PARIS ■ FRANCE]

Place Vendôme is the second of the two Parisian squares ordered by King Louis XIV, who went down in history as "Louis the Great " or "the Sun King ", and are evidence of the sovereign's desire to celebrate himself as the true symbol of France. When Cardinal Mazarin died in 1661, Louis XIV (who had come to the throne in 1643, with his mother, Anne of Austria, as regent, and the guidance of Mazarin himself) assumed all powers and initiated his own personal policies, relying on the collaboration of able, devoted ministers, including Jean-Baptiste Colbert for the economy, and François Michel Le Tellier de Louvois, who reorganized the army.

The square, whose name derives from the supposed presence of the residence of the Duke of Vendôme, the illegitimate son of Henry IV, was designed in 1685, together with Place des Victoires, by the same person: Jules Hardouin Mansart, the most famous and respected architect of the time. The model for the two new urban installations was the tried and tested *place royale*, inaugurated by Henry IV and here renewed by the obvious monumentality that resorts explicitly to the style repertoire of classical architecture. The inflexible geometrical layout of Place des Vosges, was, in fact, closely associated to the buildings that defined it and conceived as part of a "modular" iteration logic, which became fundamental in the development of Baroque urban design. Consequently, individual buildings were no longer conceived as isolated elements, but as pertaining to an overall urban-planning scale of dimensions, contributing to the design by the repetition of building modules

and laid out in accordance with a scenographic plan that valorized monumental aspects. In this respect, Place Vendôme still stands as one of the most comprehensive expressions of seventeenth-century French urban planning, whose roots can be seen in Place des Vosges and, at the same time, shows the close link existing between French Baroque and Classicism, which was already being implemented in 1667 by Claude Perrault in his construction of the Louvre's eastern facade.

Initial designs for Place Vendôme envisaged construction of a square plaza with buildings on three sides, open to the south and with prestigious installations: libraries, embassies, even the State Mint. Building began in 1696, tracing out the perimeter of the square, starting with façades that would be endowed with standard style and decoration features. The actual buildings were to have been built at a later date, after the plots of land had been sold. In 1699, as work went ahead and a statue of the Louis XIV on horseback (dressed as a Roman Emperor) had already been erected, the King changed his mind and demanded the square become octagonal. So the architect opted for a rectangle with cut-off corners, opening the square both to the north and the south, thereby connecting it to Rue Saint-Honoré and Rue des Capucines. During the Revolution, the statue of the King was destroyed and, in 1810, Napoleon ordered the Colonne Vendôme to be built, in imitation of Trajan's Column in Rome. Around the spiral shaft he decided to install a series of 66 bas reliefs made from the molten bronze from the 1,200 cannons captured during his victory at Austerlitz. The bas reliefs were designed by Pierre-Nolasque Bergeret, and commemorate the 1805-07 victories of the "small emperor".

76-77 and 78-79 ■ **The spectacular setting of Place Vendôme, based on the Place Royale model, shows a monumental succession of identical buildings that form an continuous and balanced building curtain.**

77 ■ **Jules Hardouin Mansart, great-nephew and pupil of François Mansart, was appointed Royal Architect in 1685. He became one of the most famous and sought-after French architects, and also designed the extensions into the gardens and the chapel at Versailles Palace, as well as the Dôme des Invalides, in Paris.**

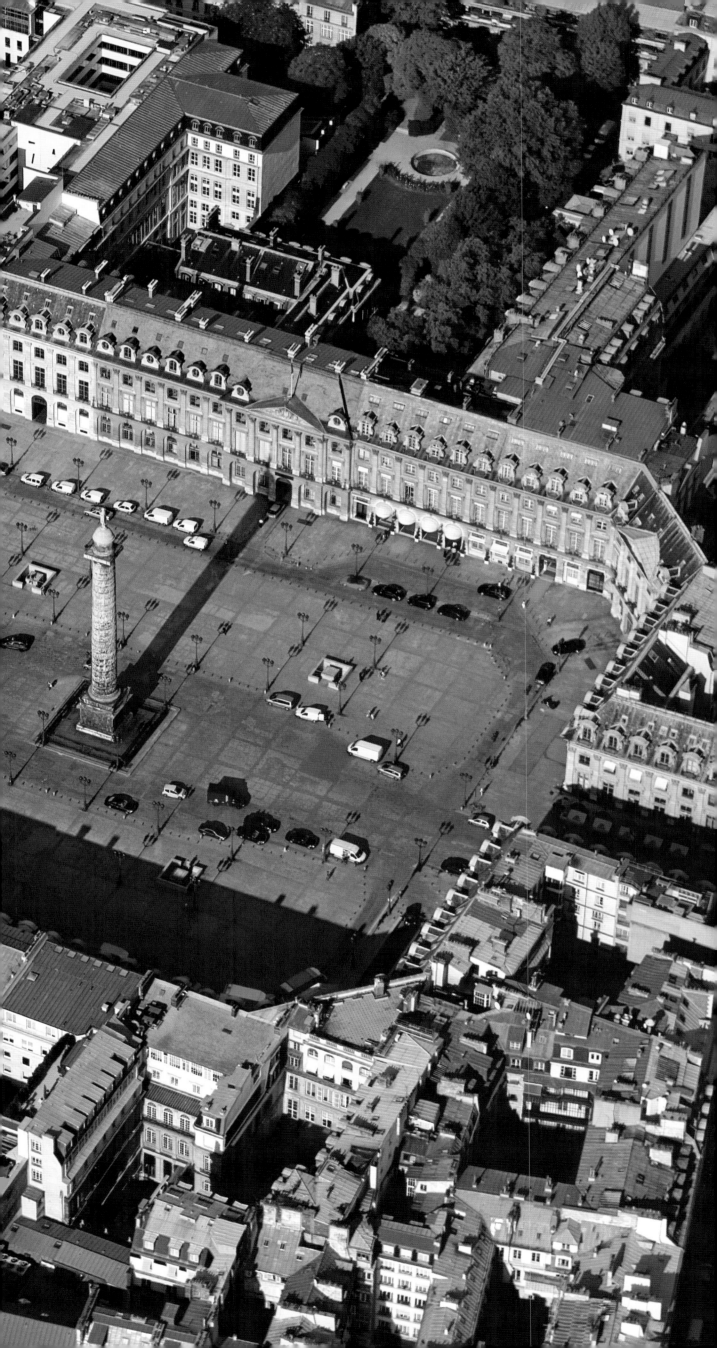

Although the square preserved its rectangular plan and architectural design, it became a thorough-fare when Rue de Castiglione and Rue de la Paix were opened, and, ruined by heavy traffic lost its quiet atmosphere. In 1991, the Conseil de Paris decided to abolish unmanageable parking, seeking inspiration in Mansart's 1699 project. Pierre Prunet, the architect appointed for the scheme, produced a modern interpretation of the primary indications, without effect on the site's current constraints: traffic continues to flow from north to south, with space circumscribed and pedestrians finding easy access around the shopping area, as well as tidying up the appearance of paths and urban furnishings. Today, Place Vendôme is a single paved area that ideally suggests the sandy surface thought of by Mansart; traffic is channeled to the spaces that the seventeenth-century architect intended as trotting tracks, and these have also been redesigned and delimited by elegant stainless steel bollards. The paving is a geometrical grid: earth-colored bands of granite create twenty-by-twenty foot (6 x 6m) squares whose proportions derive from the base of the Colonne Vendôme. The occupied area is thus given a new order which discreetly merges with that of the building façades, whose seventeenth-century design is untouched: the ashlar ground floor opens into a series of arches overlaid by a double order of windows, united by giant Corinthian pilaster strips and mansard roofs. The chamfered corners and the center line of the "modules" on the long sides are gabled to break up the sequence of dormer windows.

Place Vendôme is still an expression of the immense opulence insisted upon by the Sun King; and it is not surprising that it should share its location with the world's most prestigious jewelers, Cartier and Van Cleef, the exclusive Hôtel Ritz, the Ministry of Justice, which occupies two period *hôtels particuliers*, and art collections and famous stores.

80 ■ The Vendôme column, replacing the previous statue of Louis XIV, removed during the French Revolution, now stands in the center of the square. The column, however, was erected by Napoleon mimicking the example of Trajan's column in Rome, intending to commemorate his own imperial victories from 1805 to 1807.

81 ■ Like the Trajan column, the Colonne Vendôme is also decorated with a series of 66 bas reliefs that spiral around its shaft; the reliefs are by Pierre-Nolasque Bergeret and were cast from the bronze of the 1,200 cannons captured after the victory at Austerlitz. The Emperor Napoleon is portrayed at the top.

LOCATION	YEAR OF CONSTRUCTION	AREA	APPLICATION	STYLE
PARIS (FRANCE)	1685, 1696-1699, 1991	187,000 SQ FEET	CIVIC SQUARE	BAROQUE

PLACE DES
TERREAUX

[LYON ■ FRANCE]

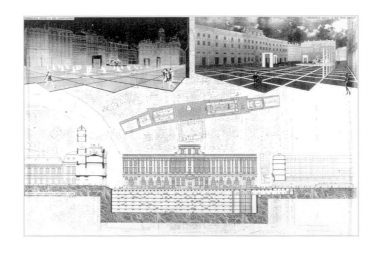

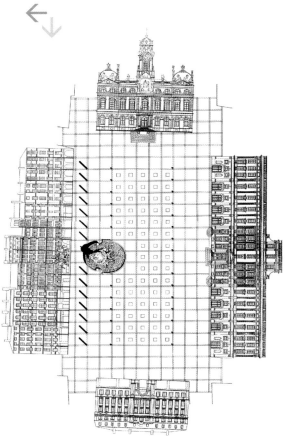

82-83 ■ Cafés bordering the monumental fountain in front of the Palais Saint Pierre.

83 ■ The square shown in a design by Christian Drevet and Daniel Buren, conceiving a way of intervening in its redevelopment, flanking it with the profiles of the buildings set around the perimeter.

Historically the center of urban life in Lyon, Place des Terreaux became an image of the success achieved by the Grand Lyon policy in the 1990s, whose upgrading of public space was methodically used to restore a sense of identity to the contemporary city. The square has, in fact, a monumental nature, expressing as it does the representative requirements of the municipality, religious authorities, and lastly the middle classes, which materialized respectively in the Hôtel de Ville, Palais Saint Pierre (now Musée des Beaux Arts, but in the 1600s the Abbey of Saint Pierre) and the Massif des Terreaux. The square is in the heart of Presqu'île, the alluvial cone that originated at the confluence of the rivers Rhône and Saône, and thus separated from the old city, which is set on the hill that slopes down to the River Saône, and from the modern city, which extends along the banks of the Rhône.

The seventeenth century was a crucial historical period for the development of the square: the area was paved and the buildings that then defined its plan were erected.

82 bottom ■ The section of the square shows the five underground levels used for the construction of car parks, and the façade of the Palais Saint Pierre. The section is surrounded images of the square's layout and perspectives.

84 ■ Frédéric Auguste Bartholdi's monumental Fountain of the Rivers is set against the façade of the Hôtel de Ville.

84-85 ■ The charm of this square is skillfully expressed by the illuminated and dancing fountains that transform it into a shimmering sheer carpet.

The same buildings continued to play a role right through to the present day, guiding the hand of architect Christian Drevet and artist Daniel Buren in their studies for the enhancement scheme. The Hôtel de Ville, by Simon Maupin, was built between 1645 and 1651; following a fire, it was in part rebuilt in 1702 by Jules Hardouin Mansart, who had worked on Place Vendôme in Paris. It is considered one of France's most handsome buildings and forms one of the square's shorter sides. After its construction, the Convent of Saint Pierre was also built in the new style, due to an intervention by François Royers de la Valfranière, which defined the long side of the rectangle that forms Place des Terreaux.

At the moment the square appears as an ample rectangular pedestrian area, accessible to vehicular traffic only on two sides, thanks to the project that resulted from teamwork between architect Drevet and artist Buren, who took inspiration from waterworks and lighting installations to breathe new life into the site, animating it both day and night. This was possible through intelligent use of paving, with a two-tone black and white scheme of granite strips that split the area into a grid of regular squares. The size of the paving strips is 20 feet (5.9 meters) and derives from that of the pilaster strips at Palais Saint Pierre, applied as the project's regulating module. The result is a pattern of 69 squares, set

LOCATION	YEAR OF CONSTRUCTION	AREA	APPLICATION	STYLE
LYON (FRANCE)	17TH CENTURY-1994	APPROXIMATELY 86,000 SQ FEET	CIVIC SQUARE	BAROQUE

slightly lower than the square itself, with waterworks that spray adjustable jets of water and form a sequence of small fountains. In the evening the fountains are lit – a charming sight. The paving strips, moreover, seem to rise where they meet the edg, to create striped cubes towards Palais Saint Pierre, whereas on the opposite side they rise to form tall pilasters that are a backdrop to the bank of *terrasse*, coffee shops that face onto the square and frame Frédéric Auguste Bartholdi's monumental fountain.

The Fontaine Bartholdi was moved from its original central position, towards the less obvious curtain wall that typifies the location, but turned to face Palais Saint Pierre, which is thus further valorized. Its symmetrical façade is the same length as the square's lengthwise side, cadenced by a double order of Doric pilaster strips on the lower levels, and Corinthian ones above, over which a baluster curves into an attic coping of the central block.

Another exceptional wing is the Hôtel de Ville, which majestically dominates one of the short sides, and whose central attic is decorated with a relief of Henry IV on horseback, with the clock tower to the rear. The upgrading project dedicated to Place des Terreaux was just one of the many works realized in Lyon's public spaces, part of a coordinated action that aimed to elevate the specificity of each site by underscoring their differences and highlighting their history.

STANISLAS

[NANCY ■ FRANCE]

Place Stanislas is one of the loveliest squares in France. A masterpiece of eighteenth-century art, it was commissioned by Stanislas Leszczynski, "the king with no kingdom," and is the oldest example of the modern capital where the welfare of the citizens – meaning what we would now call easy access to services – combined with the celebration of the sovereign's power. (As King of Poland, Stanislas had been all but forced to abdicate; his son-in-law, King Louis XV of France, conferred on him the Duchy of Lorraine for life.)

In Nancy, Stanislas worked intensively with his favorite architect, Emmanuel Héré de Corny, to create a new style for the capital, while simultaneously celebrating his son-in-law for the help he had given him. When Stanislas became Duke of Lorraine in 1736, Nancy was split into two sections: the old city and the new, created by Charles III in 1588, and separated by a huge area of flat ground that the military commander of the stronghold deemed indispensable for strategic reasons. It was this stretch of ground that became Place Stanislas and eventually gave the whole city a different appearance.

A great number of difficulties had to be overcome between planning and realizing the project, and it was only in 1752 that the first stone was laid to begin paving the square. In 1756 the solemn inauguration of Place Royale, now Stanislas, took place, the first of the three royal squares that the Duke ordered: Place de la Carrière, Place d'Alliance, and the most famous – the one named after him. Together, the three form a truly interesting complex, not only because of their mon-

86 ■ The Arc de Triomphe's attic commemorates King Louis XV, to whom Stanislaus was very attached: a seated Minerva, flanked by allegorical figures, holds the marble medallion dedicated to the French sovereign.

87 ■ The monument dedicated to Stanislaus Leszczynski, erected in 1831, in the square named after him, commemorates this "king without a kingdom" who made Nancy capital of the Lorraine region in the 18th century. Stanislaus commissioned architect Emmanuel Héré de Corny to design Place Royal, now Place Stanislas.

HOSTIUM TERROR,
FŒDERUM CULTOR,
GENTISQUE DECUS ET AMOR

STANISLAS
LESZCZYNSKI
ROI DE POLOGNE
DUC
DE LORRAINE
ET
DE BAR
1737 - 1766

LOCATION	YEAR OF CONSTRUCTION	AREA	APPLICATION	STYLE
NANCY (FRANCE)	1752-1756	APPROXIMATELY 75,350 SQ FEET	CIVIC SQUARE	FROM LATE BAROQUE TO NEOCLASSICISM

umental layout, but also because they were designed in such a fashion as to facilitate citizens' access to their city's most significant venues of public life. Then, as now, the three squares led to the Hôtel de Ville (city hall), the Palace of Justice, the Palais de l'Intendance, the Collège de Médecine (now the Museum of Fine Arts), the Theater, the Botanical Gardens, and the Library.

Héré conceived a harmonious backdrop of symmetrical buildings to surround Place Royale: all share a classical order, and all are finished with balconies, whereas a series of artistic wrought iron and brass railings, by Jean Lamour, connect the buildings both symbolically and physically. These elegant railings frame the two fountains of Amphitrite and Neptune, by Barthelémy Guibal and Paul-Louis Cyfflé, at the northern corners of the square. Originally, the center was installed with a bronze statue of Louis XV in historical costume, surrounded by allegorical figures. During the French Revolution, however, the monument was destroyed. It was replaced in 1831 by a statue in honor of Stanislas, the "enlightened" ruler who did so much for Nancy. The southern side of the square is closed by the Hôtel de Ville, with its upper balcony and central tympanum bearing Stanislas' coat of arms and the insignia of the city.

The Musée des Beaux Arts is installed in one of the buildings on the west side, and to the north is an impressive triumphal arch by Héré, erected in 1752 to celebrate the glo-

88-89 ■ The view shows the statue honoring Stanislaus Leszczynski, set in the center of the square, and outlined by the symmetrical layout of the buildings around it.

89 bottom ■ The fountains of Amphitrite and Neptune elegantly link the constructions on the square. In 1771 the two side passages were opened by the Fountain of Amphitrite to allow better access to the park at the back.

ries of King Louis XV, of whom Stanislas was very fond. The arch connects to Place de la Carrière, whose current layout is still that originally designed by Héré: it connects Place Stanislas and the Hôtel de Ville to the Palais du Gouvernement, also built by the architect, from 1751 to 1753.

Nowadays the square is pedestrian precinct and has recovered its ancient splendor thanks to a successful restoration of the railings and decorative elements, as well as new paving completed in 2005. Their pale color was chosen for the brilliance it casts overall, and is highlighted by two crossing diagonals of black that break up the uniformity of the "total light" and give the space a certain cadence; in addition, numerous cafés with outdoor tables welcome visitors to the square and offer a unique setting for relaxing in a 1700s-style salon.

PLAZA
MAYOR

[MADRID ▪ SPAIN]

As Plaza Mayor's name suggests, this impressive square is very large – actually one of the biggest in Europe. It was commissioned and planned by the Hapsburg branch of the Spanish monarchy with the intention of using it to leave their dynastic stamp on the city. Previously the piazza was a shapeless space whose main feature was a strong slope down to Calle de Toledo, and was known as Plaza del Arrabal ("the suburban square"), since it lay on the outskirts of Madrid's fortified walls. This designation dates back to the fifteenth century, during the reign of Juan II, when the area was selected to act as a marketplace to avoid paying duties on all goods that entered the city.

Conceptually, Plaza Mayor was the result of a scheme put forward by King Philip II, who

commissioned Juan de Herrera, architect of El Escorial, to design a new, vast piazza that would

upgrade the market area and eliminate the natural slope from the terrain. Thus began the expropriation of existing buildings, and the leveling of the area, but the project was never completed, since the plans for it were lost in a fire. Only Antonio Sillero's Casa de la Panadería of 1590, and the Casa de la Carniceria of the same period, were completed. They were the only two public buildings of the entire complex; the rest of the complex was intended to be residential. When Philip III succeeded to the throne of Spain, he ordered Juan Gómez de Mora, the trusted architect who had been delegated to manage all of Madrid's main building sites, to complete construction. Plaza Mayor was officially inaugurated on May 15, 1620, concurrently with celebrations for San Isidro, and from that moment its massive size and regular layout made it the venue of choice for every public event of the day, from

90-91 ■ Plaza Mayor expresses a concept of unity mirrored in the regularity of the buildings around its perimeter, with the exception of Casa de la Panadería, demarcated by two vertical tower elements and covered in frescoes.

REYNANDO
CARLOSIIGOB
ERNANDODO
NAMARYANA
SVMADRE167ᵃ

PLAZA
MAYOR

RESTAURADA
AÑO
MDCCCLXXXI

92-93 ■ **The lavish frescoes and huge armorial bearings decorating Casa de
la Panadería are the backdrop to the monument to Philip III, the monarch
who contributed to completion of the square.**

executions ordered by the Holy Inquisition to performances of Lope de Vega's religious
plays, and even to bullfights.

Plaza Mayor was seriously damaged by a fire in 1790 and subsequently refurbished by
Juan de Villanueva. He introduced the arches that now demarcate the square's incoming
access streets, and decreased the maximum height of buildings like Casa de la Panadería
from six to four stories.

In 1848, an equestrian monument dedicated to Philip III (begun by Giambologna and finished by his pupil Pietro Tacca in 1613) was installed in the center of the plaza. It was
around this time (the mid-nineteenth century) that the market disappeared, due to the
abolition of duties, and that the square began to attract the businesses it has still today, such as stores, craft workshops, and cafés.

Plaza Mayor has always been characterized by its impeccable geometrical plan: it is a
large rectangle that stands out from the dense network of irregular blocks that make
up the *barrio bajo*, Madrid's medieval quarter. Its perimeter stops short the maze of

LOCATION	YEAR OF CONSTRUCTION	AREA	APPLICATION	STYLE
MADRID (SPAIN)	MID-1500s – 1620	130,525 SQ FEET	CIVIC SQUARE	BAROQUE

streets that surrounds it, and does so (thanks to Villanueva's interventions) with two-story arches the span the eight streets leading into it. All the buildings around it are defined by a ground level arcade set on architraved pilasters, except for Casa de la Panaderia, whose portico comprises semi-columns set against pilasters supporting round arches. The three residential floors above the ground floor have smooth, monochromatic plaster façades, cadenced by the iteration of ample french windows that open on long balconies, while the Casa de la Panadería façade stands out for the numerous frescoes and the two vertical tower elements that demarcate it.

In reality, the morphology of Plaza Mayor is not so much Spanish in flavor as reminiscent of the French *place royale* concept, based as it is on a rigorous geometry underscored by uniformity of building elevations. The traces of the ancient leveling of the terrain are no longer visible, but hidden by the paving that divides the area into brick, white and gray-colored squares; and these are in turn hidden daily by the feet of the countless citizens and visitors who crowd this veritable oasis in the middle of Madrid.

SCHLOSSPLATZ

[STUTTGART ■ GERMANY]

Stuttgart's famed Schlossplatz, or Castle Square, plays a crucial role in the life of the Baden-Württemberg capital. Comprised of a large garden dominated by the eighteenth-century residence created by Italian architect Leopoldo Retti, this lovely site is a favorite destination for local residents, tourists, and art lovers, thanks to the pleasant atmosphere created by its lawns and flowerbeds (and its proximity to the main railway station) and the site of of several regional authorities.

94-95 ■ The view shows the vast Schlossplatz space, crossed by radial pathways interspersed with flowerbeds and plants, with the square occupying the same area as the Neues Schloss that overlooks it.

The square is named after the Neues Schloss, or "new castle"; that is, the building commissioned by Duke Karl Eugen von Württemberg from Retti, the nephew of Donato Frisoni, who had designed the much-admired Baroque Ludwigsburg residence. The complex was marked "new" to distinguish it from the old castle – the Altes Schloss – which still stands not far away, its towering façades facing both Schlossplatz and the older Schillerplatz, which partially hides it from view.

The erection of the Neues Schloss began in 1746 and developed around a central block and two wings, imitating the model used for Versailles, and surrounding a great court that borders today's square along the entire east side. The death of the architect did not pre-

96 ■ Twin fountains, set at the sides of the Jubilee Column, embellish the square with its flowerbeds.

96-97 ■ The Jubilee Column, in the center of the square, is aligned with the main Neues Schloss entrance, and was erected in 1841, for the 25th anniversary of Wilhelm I's accession to the throne.

98-99 ■ At night dancing fountains and lights enhance the charm of what is beyond any doubt Stuttgart's most beautiful square.

vent continuation of the work, and it was passed on to Philippe de la Guêpière a decade after the site had begun. This architect added a cupola element to the central block and completed the section towards the garden, flanking the building. A destructive fire, here shifted the Duke's attention to the Ludwigsburg construction, however; and repairs on the damaged Neues Schloss did not proceed until 1782, under the direction of Reinhard F. H. Fischer. Later, with the proclamation of the Kingdom of Württemberg, in 1806, the interiors were entrusted to Nikolaus Thouret.

(After devastating bombings in 1944, during World War II, the entire exterior of the complex had to be rebuilt. This project was undertaken from 1958 to 1965, using original designs; meanwhile, the interiors were configured applying modern-day criteria.)

The north side of the plaza is occupied by the Königsbau, built by order of King Wilhelm I to balance the Neues Schloss. The structure had a dual function: to complete the entertainment spaces for court events and to offer a shopping arcade of sorts. It was designed from 1842 to 1846 by Johann M. Knapp, and developed by Christian Leins. (It too had to be rebuilt after World War II, as did Aberlin Tretsch's sixteenth-century Altes Schloss, which faces it on the south side of the square.)

On the west side stands the plaza's most recent building, the monumental Kunstgebäude, designed from 1909 to 1913 by Theodor Fischer to host art exhibitions and collections. It was rebuilt in the 1950s, too, by Paul Bonatz, who was Fischer's pupil and who respected the original plan, which was

LOCATION	YEAR OF CONSTRUCTION	AREA	APPLICATION	STYLE
STUTTGART (GERMANY)	18TH-20TH CENTURY	APPROXIMATELY 312,000 SQ FEET	CIVIC SQUARE	STRATIFIED LATE BAROQUE TO HISTORICISM

rectangular around a circular hall with cupola, preceded by a portico of renaissance inspiration.

Like Dresden's Theaterplatz, Schlossplatz is a winning rejoinder to the destruction suffered by Germany in World War II, and a testament to its tenacity in recovering the symbols of an important historical chapter. Although the walls of the Altes Schloss still bear shrapnel damage, the onlooker will have the over-all impression that nothing ever happened. The elegant lines of the Neues Schloss's triple-order façade was the prelude to the onset of Classicism, whereas the layout and the window cornices declare the building's Late Baroque intentions. It is a perfect backdrop to the lawns that intersperse the paving, encircling two huge fountains and the Jubiläumsräume, a column erected in 1841 to celebrate the 25th anniversary of Wilhelm I's acceptance of the monarchy.

On the other side, the square is completed by the balanced sequence of round arches of the Italian – inspired Kunstgebäude, now the venue for temporary exhibitions and a permanent collection of the works of Otto Dix. Lastly, the Königsbau's austere Ionic colonnade cadences the prospect from the exhibition center gallery to the regional offices in the Neues Schloss, evoking the *stoà* spirit of Ancient Greece.

PLAZA DE LA
CONSTITUCIÓN

[MEXICO CITY ■ MEXICO]

One of the biggest plazas in the world, in terms of size, the vast Plaza de la Constitución is where the first Mexican constitution was declared, in 1813. Today it is still used for official ceremonies, entertainment events, and national celebrations. It is known, locally, as Zócalo, which means "plinth," since a monument to commemorate independence was to have been installed there, but this plan was never implemented. Nonetheless, the word came into common usage, with the odd result that not just this plaza, but many other squares in Mexico, are known as Zócalo.

The earliest nucleus of Plaza de la Constitución can be traced back to the conquest of the Aztec capital – then known as Tenochtitlán – by the Spanish conquistadors who destroyed the temples and original buildings there. One such building was the Templo Mayor, erected by the Aztecs between the fourteenth and fifteenth centuries, and whose remains were brought to light north of the plaza, following the chance discovery, in 1978, of

100-101 ■ The vast square plaza is accessed by the straight Avenida Francisco I Madero, which opens onto the façade of Palacio Nacional, seat of presidential offices.

101 ■ The Metropolitan Cathedral occupies one side of the square, together with the neighboring Sagrario Metropolitano, distinguished by the multitude of statues that decorate the façades. Two tall towers are set one at each side of the main church façade.

the Stone of Coyolxauhqui, a giant monolith named after the goddess of the moon. Montezuma's palace, on the other hand, was initially retained and used as a residence by Hernán Cortés after the conquest of Mexico, but was later replaced by today's Palacio Nacional, which forms one side of the square. This extensive complex dates back to the sixteenth century (with later modifications) and is the location of the President's offices. It alone constitutes half an entire block. The ancient archbishopric is next to it, across the road to Moneda.

Zócalo is dominated by the sculptural silhouette of the Metropolitan Cathedral, Latin America's biggest church, and the core of one of the most populous dioceses in the world. The impressive building, initiated in the seventeenth century on the remains of a previous small church, required many years to be brought to completion, and the site lingered for another two hundred years, until 1813. Next to it stands the eighteenth-century Sagrario Metropolitano, used as a parish church serving the cathedral, and next to that, the Monte de Piedad. The latter is a Renaissance building, standing opposite Palacio Nacional, and is one of the oldest installations in the square, though it is now flanked with new buildings that house restaurants, shops, and hotels, including the Gran Hotel and the Hotel Majestic, whose terrace offers a splendid view of the square. Other public buildings erected opposite the cathedral include the old and new city halls and, at the edge, the Supreme Courts.

LOCATION	YEAR OF CONSTRUCTION	AREA	APPLICATION	STYLE
MEXICO CITY (MEXICO)	12TH-19TH CENTURY	620,000 SQ FEET	RELIGIOUS AND CIVIC SQUARE	STRATIFIED RENAISSANCE TO LATE BAROQUE

Plaza de la Constitución is still a vast paved area at whose center the Mexican flag flies on a tall mast against the backdrop of the Palacio Nacional's large façade in quarried grey stone and volcanic red stone. The three stories of the building are closed at either end by two towers, while its width is marked by three entrance blocks capped with tympanums and called Puerta Mariana, after President Mariano Arista who ordered its creation, Puerta Centrale, and Puerta de Honor, which is used by the presidents. Inside, the courtyards feature three orders of loggias with ashlar arches. The main staircase is decorated with a mural by Diego Rivera, painted from 1929 to 1935, and dedicated to the country's turbulent history.

The forms of the cathedral testify to numerous episodic transformations – that is, the stratified layers of the

102-103 ■ The square's vastness is immediately perceived in relation to the majestic proportions of the Metropolitan Cathedral and the Palacio Nacional, which delineate two of its sides; the Mexican flag is raised in the center of the area.

103 bottom ■ Plaza de
la Constitución, or Zócalo,
as it is known, because of
the plinth of a monument
commemorating the
country's independence
and most likely installed
there in the early 19th
century.

church speak of an evolving style from Renaissance to Late Baroque. Two monumental belfries

housing eighteen bells hug the ornate façade, behind which lies a nave and four aisles. Next to

this are the Sagrario's ultra-sculpted front, decked with countless statues of saints, and (be-

hind the Sagrario) a garden containing the Fuente de la Zona Lacustre, reminiscent of the city's

origins, bearing the map of the old Aztec capital of Tenochtitlán.

On the south side,
the square plaza opens
onto the River Tagus, with
the two long parallelepiped
buildings, called the
"Torreoes", reaching
riverwards and forming
the east and west side
of the square.

PRAÇA DO
COMÉRCIO

[LISBON ■ PORTUGAL]

Today's Praça do Comércio (Commerce Square) owes its origins to a dramatic occurrence: the terrible 1755 earthquake and the devastating fire that followed. Prior to these events it was a large open space called Terreiro do Paço – in other words, "Palace Terrace" – along the right bank of the Tagus, where the Paço da Ribeira ("river palace") had been built in the early sixteenth century, and then modified several times, until 1775, when it was totally destroyed by the earthquake. Portugal's head government minister at the time was the Marquis Pombal, an erudite, strong-willed man, steeped in Illuminist theories, who enjoyed the fullest trust of the King, José I.

And it was on account of this trust that the Marquis was able to promote the creation of a new Lisbon in the remarkably short period of only a few years.

Naturally it helped that the destruction caused by the earthquake was terrible and complete, allowing for a radical modification of the urban fabric in the section where Rossio

– that is to say Praça Dom Pedro IV – now starts, passing through Baixa, the commercial district, to reach the river through the monumental Praça do Comércio. Thus two squares were constructed, connected by wide, straight streets intersected at right angles by side streets that replaced the previous maze of pathways. This urban plan was mainly inspired by the military engineer, Manuel da Maia, and realized by the architects Eugenio dos Santos and Carlos Mardel.

Studies for modification of the Terreiro do Paço area and its hinterland had already begun before the earthquake, precisely because Pombal wanted to bring to Lisbon the innovations suggested by new Illuminist culture. It had been difficult to make progress, however, because of the need for massive expropriation and the limitations imposed by existing constructions. The way was finally cleared, however, when the quake and the ensuing chaos it brought aabout made it possible to build from scratch. Prior to November 1755, what is now a vast square was an irregular rectangle, whose size was about 877 feet along the north side and 375 feet along the west side, with a 260-foot east side and a 765-foot south side, towards the Tagus. So instructions that the engineer da Maia gave to dos Santos and the other site foremen were very precise and aimed to rationalize the existing situation: in the case of the square, for example, it was decided to make each side about 585 feet, to achieve a square plan.

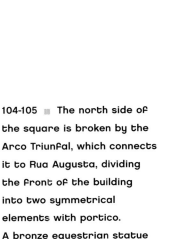

104-105 ■ The north side of the square is broken by the Arco Triunfal, which connects it to Rua Augusta, dividing the front of the building into two symmetrical elements with portico. A bronze equestrian statue of the sovereign Dom José I is in the center of the square.

LOCATION	YEAR OF CONSTRUCTION	AREA	APPLICATION	STYLE
LISBON (PORTUGAL)	1756 ONWARDS	APPROXIMATELY 330,000 SQ FEET	CIVIC SQUARE	NEOCLASSICAL

Moreover, as the new royal palace was not going to be rebuilt, da Maia suggested moving the Stock Exchange there, and he was supported by the Lisbon Chamber of Commerce, and the issuance of royal authorization shortly after that, in January 1758. This effective interest shown by the merchant class influenced the name selected for the square: in fact, unlike other major European cities, whose impressive urban spaces were at this time in history, dedicated to national or dynastic rulers as a matter of course, Lisbon dedicated its new center to the mercantile trade that had allowed its resurrection. Nonetheless, almost as a compensation, the equestrian statue of Dom José I was set in the center of the square, where it is still to be seen, and four new streets that connect the Rossio with Praça do Comércio were named after members of the royal family. The bronze statue, a masterpiece by Joaquim Machado de Castro, stands on a tall plinth bearing the royal insignia and a medallion depicting the Marquis Pombal, with the allegories of Fame and Triumph decorating the sides.

The large, square plaza opens onto the River Tagus to the south, with the opposite side filled by four porticoed blocks that house ministries and public offices designed by dos Santos; they have survived without significant changes. The two central buildings, separated from

106-107 ■ The sequence of buildings defining the Praça do Comércio's vast space were designed with a series of ground floor porticoes and regular openings on the higher floors, ending in an elegant balustrade that confers unity and harmony to the plaza.

Rua Augusta by the Arco Triunfal, are supported by a system of round arch porticoes – 11 arches altogether – which continue into the smaller, neighboring buildings, separated by Rua Aurea and Rua da Prata. As a result, the backdrop formed by the central triumphal arch is heavily underscored, while the recurring massive sustaining pilasters in the portico create overall harmony. The sides perpendicular to the estuary are completed by two long paral-lelepipeds, called Torreoes and closed, riverwards, by two towers designed by the Italian Filippo Terzi, who paid homage to those that existed before the earthquake, and which were ordered by Felipe II to complete the building. The Arco Triunfal soars tall and majestic to the north, ini-tiated during the reconstruction but not finished until 1873, almost a century later. The sup-porting structure is understated, comprising pilasters surrounded by classical columns, while the attic is lavishly decorated and closes with the allegory of Glory crowning Genius and Valor. The square's most fascinating point is to the south, facing the Tagus: onlookers raising their eyes to the hillside will observe the castle that dominates other buildings and the gently slop-ing Baixa, while a glance at the large estuary will focus on the 25the of April Suspension Bridge, which links the two banks. It is precisely midway down the south side of Praça do Comércio that the old landing stage was marked by two columns, removed in 1998 to allow restoration of the jetty. This old structure is a reminder that Terreiro do Paço, before becoming the recent square, was actually the "noble" gateway to the city of Lisbon, which was always reached by water. Now the historical wharf has been replaced by a new mooring for the ferries that con-nect the administrative and historical part to the residential and industrial, more modern area of Lisbon. This quarter, ruined for many years by chaotic traffic and parking spaces, has now been freed of cars and restored with its former charm, so it is a pleasure to linger in the cafes and admire the river and surrounding terraces of buildings.

TRAFALGAR
SQUARE

[LONDON ■ UNITED KINGDOM]

Dominated by the statue of Admiral Horatio Nelson and the National Gallery, Trafalgar Square is a huge plaza right in the center of London, not far from Piccadilly Circus, although the order of its composition and its monumental appearance make it seem quite distant. In reality, both squares were designed by the same man, the great British architect John Nash, who became a protégé of the Prince Regent, George IV, after the enormous success of his designs for Regent's Park and Regent Street. Subsequently he was appointed to undertake further urban interventions in the heart of the city, with the intention of liberating the British Museum from its Bloomsbury isolation and connecting it to the areas he had already developed. Nash imagined what was later to become Trafalgar Square as the suitable arrival point for the avenue called Whitehall, where

108-109 ■ The aerial view shows the square's new structure, no longer stifled by the traffic, thanks to Norman Foster's upgrading, completed in 2003.

109 ■ The statue of Admiral Nelson, atop a 145-foot granite Corinthian column, is 20 feet tall.

it meets the Strand, but above all he intended it to connect with Bloomsbury, proposing a wide, straight line that skirted St. Martin's Lane and would meet with an extended Coventry Street east of Piccadilly.

Plans for St. Martin's Lane were never implemented, however, and development of Tottenham Court Road and Charing Cross Road further excluded the British Museum from the West End. What did emerge was Trafalgar Square, retaining on one side the classical pronaos of St. Martin in the Fields, and the central installation of a new bank and a monument to Admiral Nelson celebrating his famous naval victory. The equestrian statue of Charles I, a seventeenth-century work by the French artist Hubert le Seur, was safeguarded, and over the years other statues dedicated to George IV and generals Charles James Napier and Henry Havelock were added at the corners of the square, each on its own plinth.

Although the urban design of Trafalgar Square is attributable to Nash, the architectural design is mainly the work of Charles Barry, with interventions by Robert Smirke, Herbert Baker, and Edwin Lutyens, who realized, respectively, Canada House (1824-27), South Africa House (1933) and the fountains (1939) that surround Nelson's Column.

Trafalgar Square was once the site of the royal stables, but they were demolished to make way for the building of the National Gallery (1831) – the result of a resolution by Parliament after the press mocked a planned conversion of the structure into a private res-

idence. The square was enhanced with a magnificent new classical building, set on a tall foundation, designed by William Wilkins; and the Gallery itself was extended several times, most recently by the addition of the Sainsbury Wing, which was designed by the American firm Venturi, Rauch, and Scott Brown and completed in 1991.

Trafalgar Square has always been busy as the destination of art enthusiasts and tourists, but for years it suffered from uneven use, since it was merely crossed to reach a small pedestrian area on the south side, towards Whitehall, where visitors crowded to get the best views for photographs, despite risking fast traffic. In fact, Trafalgar Square acted as a huge roundabout until 2003, when the north side was entrusted (by Transport for London Street Management) to Norman Foster's prestigious British firm, who had won a competition, and turned into a pedestrian precinct. Today, as a result, the square has a new layout, thanks to the research carried out by Foster and London University's Space Syntax Laboratory.

The pedestrian area was extended to embrace that point to the south where tourists linger for their photographs, which is also where Charles I on horseback may be admired – the same statue that observed the foundation of Trafalgar Square. The existing road to the north, in front of the National

110-111 ■ The monumental National Gallery, the work of William Wilkins, and the church of St. Martin in the Fields, form the backdrop to one of the multilobed fountains designed by Sir Edwin Lutyens.

110 bottom ■ Four bronze lions, each approximately 20 feet long, were cast from the bronze of French cannons, to a design by Edwin Landseer.

111 ■ The painting shows the 1863 parade that took place for wedding of Edward, Prince of Wales, to Princess Alexandra.

Gallery entrance, has been closed and its bed now replaced by a wide staircase aligned with the building, which valorizes the Gallery's monumental Ionic pronaos and two trademark wings; these now look out onto a panoramic terrace enclosed by balusters and connected to the historic plaza. Below the terrace, on either side of the ramp, several service areas act as further links between the important art gallery and life in the square outside: coffee shops, rest rooms, and lifts for the disabled so that they can travel from ground level directly to the Gallery entrance. To fit in with the architectural context, the new structures have an understated design and, where possible, reuse materials and methods derived from the demolished supporting wall, integrated with York stone, granite, and steel.

The terrace of the National Gallery offers easily accessible views of Lutyens' two multi-lobed fountains, and between them, though slightly forward, Nelson's Column, with its 145 feet (44 meters) of bronze statue. The granite column is supported by a plinth decorated with reliefs said to have been cast from the bronze of French cannons, and are flanked by Edwin Landseer's four enormous lions. Three of the four plinths installed at the corners of the square are occupied by the statues of George IV, Charles James Napier, and Henry Havelock, while the fourth offers temporary exhibition space to works by contemporary artists, chosen by a special commission. The Neoclassical prospect of Canada House and renewed 1900s Classicism of South Africa House, both of which are embassies, complete the west and east sides of the square, alongside the eighteenth-century pronaos of St. Martin in the Fields.

LOCATION	YEAR OF CONSTRUCTION	AREA	APPLICATION	STYLE
LONDON (UNITED KINGDOM)	1820-1840 – 1996-2003	APPROXIMATELY 130,000 SQ FEET	CIVIC SQUARE	STRATIFIED NEOCLASSICISM TO CONTEMPORARY

112 top ■ The front elevation of Schinkel's
Schauspielhaus expresses the extreme
simplicity of the building erected.

112 bottom ■ The Schauspielhaus' grave,
understated solidity stands out in the
center of the Gendarmenmarkt.

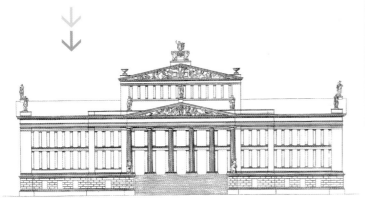

GENDARMENMARKT

[BERLIN ■ GERMANY]

A regal image of 1800s Berlin, Gendarmenmarkt survived the serious damage it sustained during World War II bombardments and retains the balanced and harmonious interaction of volume that has always defined it. Conceived during the reign of Frederick William III by the architect Karl Friedrich Schinkel in 1818, at the same time he developed the design of the new theater; it arose amid interventions that had begun with Frederick the Great, and helped the city's continued transformation into a lavish capital. Schinkel, its greatest and most successful exponent, devised a plan to refurbish the key areas of the city with new architectures that created continuity and valorized extant squares, streets, and traffic arteries.

Schinkel's work on Gendarmenmarkt gave it a sufficiently delineated layout but one not equally unitary and harmonious – a result of its eighteenth-century origins. Mapped out by grid of perpendicular streets, it became a large rectangle where the market was held, and a church was built at either end, with cemeteries destined for use, respectively, by the reformed French and German communities. To the north of the site a religious building was erected for Berlin's Huguenots, a presence in the city since 1685, and the project was en-

112-113 ■ The image shows the Gendarmenmarkt's regular, symmetrical structure, with the theater set in key position and the focal point of the urban arrangement.

trusted to Louis Cayart, who completed the work in 1705. Three years later the German church, designed by Martin Grüberg, was completed at the opposite side of the square.

In 1735, around the respective cemeteries, the Gens d'armes regiment built their stables; hence the name of the leftover space in the square. Later, Frederick the Great called on Carl von Gontard to ennoble the morphology of the two churches, taking inspiration from the cupolas of the twin buildings in Rome's Piazza del Popolo. Von Gontard worked on the façades with Georg Christian Ungerwhich, and their legacy is a striking mock-classical pronaos.

In 1774 the stables were demolished to make way for the Théâtre de la Comédie Française. This later proved to be too small, and was replaced in 1800 by the Schauspielhaus – the "German Theater" – built by Gotthard Langhans, but it was destroyed by fire in 1817.

The last intervention to make a definite impact on Gendarmenmarkt's architecture and urban plan, was to the result of Schinkel's intelligent commitment (bound by the recovery of the foundations of the previous theater, but successfully structuring the new building as the focal point of the square) to a Neoclassical sobriety that would interface with the existing Baroque elements. Bordered by Französische Strasse to the north and Mohrenstrasse to the south, and looking out over Markgrafenstrasse, the Gendarmenmarkt

stands even today as an impressive open and symmetrical space, dominated by the massive playhouse which is set on the midline, and flanked on either side by the two churches, which were redesigned to appear as identical twins.

The theater itself was conceived to give symmetry to the site, comprising a main block and two wings at the sides, cadenced by a series of windows set in series and without Classicist connotations. The two façades are crowned by classical tympana, however, which con-

LOCATION	YEAR OF CONSTRUCTION	AREA	APPLICATION	STYLE
BERLIN (GERMANY)	18TH CENTURY; 1818-1821	APPROXIMATELY 211,000 SQ FEET	RELIGIOUS AND CIVIC SQUARE	STRATIFIED BAROQUE TO NEOCLASSICISM

114-115 and 115 top ■ The classically-inspired pronaos connect the French and German cathedrals, designed by Martin Grüberg and completed by Carl von Gontard. The Schauspielhaus lies between them.

115 bottom ■ The Gendarmenmarkt comes to life during the month of December, when the traditional Christmas market is held there.

nect with the Ionic entrance pronaos and harmonize with the pronaos of the two neighboring churches, whose accentuated verticality is well offset by the theater's horizontal mass, raised on a solid base englobing the old foundations. The pointed arch cupolas of the two churches, in fact, are erected on a colonnaded Corinthian drum that stands out on the city's skyline, and at one time visually aligned with Operaplatz.

At this moment in time, the Gendarmenmarkt area is unified by the ground or "flooring," a geometrical play of nuanced grays, with a monument to Friedrich Schiller once removed by the Nazis but now restored to its central position. In December the square comes to life with the traditional Christmas market and – as it has done through its short but fraught history – connects the past to the present, and that in turn to the future.

KÖNIGSPLATZ

[MUNICH ■ GERMANY]

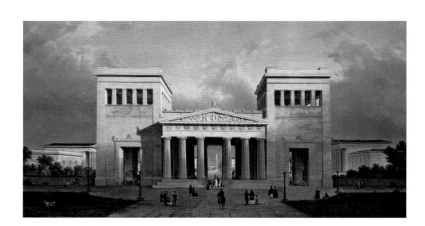

The myths of Classical Greece and admiration for Pericles' Athens seem to be under-pinnings for the civic aspirations of Ludwig I and his favorite architects Karl von Fischer, Leo von Klenze and Friedrich von Gärtner, the men who are primarily responsible for early eighteenth-century transformations to the city of Munich. In fact, they saw the city's future as one in which it would become a royal capital of Europe on a cultural par with Rome, Paris, and Vienna. Königsplatz – literally the "king's square" – is a fundamental element of one of the two great urban innovations that typify the period of Ludwig I: Ludwigstrasse

and Briennerstrasse, the two new main roads along which the city's expansion was directed to the north and to the west, with the Bavarian sovereign's residence serving as the focal point. So Königsplatz is set on Briennerstrasse, the axis that connects the royal palace to Nymphenburg Castle, and replacing the avenue that connected Munich to the monarch's summer residence.

The square was designed in neo-Grecian terms, flanked by a sculpture gallery on the north, by the young architect Karl von Fischer in about 1809-10, when he was developing the new Maxvorstadt – a planned suburb – following the 1808 competition for extending the city. Karl von Fischer died prematurely in 1820, and Königsplatz was only completed at the end of the 1840s, by Leo von Klenze, but the result was worth waiting for: a heartfelt vibrant tribute to Hellenic culture and art.

Before he died, von Fischer was able to direct works for the buildings that line the first part of Briennerstrasse and Karolinenplatz, the heart of Maxvorstadt. The thoroughfare was designed as a route cadenced by a sequence of round and square plazas ornamented with eye-catching monuments and buildings. It winds from the royal residence through the perfect circle of Karolinenplatz and finally plunges into quadrangular Königsplatz, delimited by Leo von Klenze's Propylaea, beyond which the avenue proceeds towards Stiglmaierplatz, a second round plaza, and then heads towards Nymphenburg.

To create the Glyptothek – the sculpture gallery – Ludwig I commissioned designs from several architects and rejected von Fischer's, preferring Leo von Klenze's neo-Classical sug-

116-117 The vast Königsplatz area stretches between the majestic Neoclassical Propylea, designed by the architect Leo von Klenze, and the present-day seat of the Staatliche Antikensammlungen, designed by Friedrich Ziebland.

116 bottom ■ The perspective of Leo von Klenze's Propylea mirror his love of classical architecture, shared by his patron, the sovereign, Ludwig I of Bavaria.

118 ■ The renowned Glyptothek sculpture gallery, designed by von Klenze before the Propylea, is a masterpiece of dimensions and balance which earned the architect his sovereign's admiration, setting him above the competition of his colleagues.

LOCATION	YEAR OF CONSTRUCTION	AREA	APPLICATION	STYLE
MUNICH (GERMANY)	19TH CENTURY	APPROXIMATELY 516,670 SQ FEET	CIVIC SQUARE	NEOCLASSICAL

gestion. The young architect was a pupil of Friedrich Gilly and a Berlin colleague of Karl Friedrich Schinkel who had worked with Percier and Fontaine in Paris, visited Italy and, above all, shared the king's love of classical art and was willing to express its ideals in full. In the decade 1838-1848, the Ausstellungsgebäude (exhibition hall) was erected opposite the sculpture gallery. Now home to the Staatliche Antikensammlungen (state antique collection), this art and industry building's design was entrusted to Friedrich Ziebland, while the famous Propylaea which complete the square were added from 1846 to 1862. These structures were conceived by von Klenze, who had suggested them as early as 1817, together with a church to be added opposite to balance the sculpture gallery, but the monarch did not consent to the addition of the religious building.

Currently the square retains its square plan, divided up by large areas of grass in front of the sculpture gallery to the north and the Ausstellungsgebäude to the south, while rows of trees create a backdrop. Briennerstrasse cuts through the plaza, forking near the Propylaea, bypassing them and allowing the flow of vehicle traffic, while a subway station has been installed underground. The Propylaea – the symbolic entrance to the city from the west and Nymphenburg castle – still loom impressively at the edge of the square, with the entrance framed by two tall towers and formed by weighty Doric columns that hold a sculpture-decorated fronton. They demarcate the plaza's axis, with

its symmetrical balance of the Glyptothek facing the Ausstellungsgebäude. The sculpture gallery was the first building realized on Königsplatz and is comprised of four blocks set around a square inner court. The blind façade features a series of six niches, each with a statue, arranged symmetrically along the sides of the impressive Ionic pronaos whose pediment expresses the allegorical explanation of the intention behind the creation of the structure. Today the Antikensammlungen premises are a solemn construction, also without openings, decorated by a pronaos with Corinthian columns, and a fronton with a statue of Bavaria, who holds a crown of laurel in her right hand and the scepter of good government in her left.

Königsplatz still today expresses the perfect fusion of Ludwig I's aspiration to transform Munich into the "Athens of Isar" – and his architects' ability to achieve the required effect. Today's visitor, on arriving at the square, will be impressed by the surroundings: the Doric Propylaea, similar to those that lead to the Acropolis in Athens, the Glyptothek's pure white Ionic columns, the Ausstellungsgebäude and its Corinthian pronaos. All contribute to create an ideal scenario cadenced by all three classical orders.

118-119 ■ **The Glyptothek tympanum is a declared homage to classical art and the works exhibited in the gallery.**

WINTER PALACE

SQUARE

[ST. PETERSBURG ■ RUSSIA]

120-121 ■ The view shows the Winter Palace complex in the foreground, with the vast square of the same name stretching before it, delimited by the exedra-shaped building designed by Italian architect, Carlo Rossi.

121 ■ The 155-foot column silhouetted against the majestic Triumphal Arch that celebrates the 1812 victory over Napoleon.

When in St. Petersburg, thoughts of Peter the Great and Catherine of Russia tend to linger through the endless nights of winter (or the curtailed ones of summer), especially on the Neva, at the Hermitage, and at the Winter Palace, Bartolomeo Rastrelli's masterpiece. Designed as an imperial residence, the palace is set on Winter Palace Square, whose current layout was conceived and realized by Carlo Rossi in the early 1800s. It is the crowning glory and the most complete expression of the *ex novo* city desired by Czar Peter I to demonstrate that Russia was able to meet any challenge thrown at her by the great European states. For St. Petersburg itself was created from nothing, in the early eighteenth century, at the mouth of the River Neva, in order to build a stronghold against Sweden. It was envisaged as a strategic location that would facilitate the development of relations with other European capitals, and as such it prospered rapidly, soon turning into one of Europe's loveliest and most fascinating cities.

The entire site was conceived and built on the monumental scale, without limits to means or space: Peter the Great's comfort with the colossal and his quest for magnificence were unquestioningly upheld by his successors. That quest ended in the early 1800s, when Mikhailovsky Palace Square and Winter Palace Square, as well as the theatre district, were finally completed. Winter Palace Square at once provided an impressive scenario for the Emperor's Palace, which it rolls towards, from its closed hemicycle backdrop; for its majestic dimensions frame the view of St. Isaac's Cathedral, the Senate and the Synod.

120 bottom ■ The ponderous monolith erected in Alexander I's honor, set in the center of the square, with Carlo Rossi's Triumphal Arch in the background.

LOCATION	YEAR OF CONSTRUCTION	AREA	APPLICATION	STYLE
ST. PETERSBURG (RUSSIA)	1819-1829	APPROXIMATELY 538,000 SQ FEET	CIVIC SQUARE	FROM LATE BAROQUE TO NEOCLASSICISM

The Italian architect Carlo Rossi was commissioned for the scheme and he suggested a scale that, in his opinion, would exceed the grandeur of ancient Roman buildings and ensure a result unparalleled in Europe. Before Rossi's intervention the plaza had an irregular shape, distinguished by its jagged outline and absence of harmony, betraying the lack of any clear intention to unify the built-up area. Consequently the architect, perceiving the scope of the task at hand and perhaps inspired by the layout of Naples' Piazza del Plebiscito (at that time called Piazza Reale), realized a huge exedra on the same axis as the Winter Palace, large enough to embrace its entire prospect and thereby generating the impression of a space closed by the palace's own façade.

The entrance to Bolshaja Morskaja, the wide curving avenue that accesses the square, was preserved and emphasized by including it in a lavish triumphal arch that is the kingpin of the entire intervention. Its colossal exedra is as long as the entire southern side and as wide as the front of the Winter Palace. In 1834, a sturdy column – the biggest monolith in the world, intended to honor Alexander I – was erected at the center of the square, shifting focus from the triumphal arch that had previously been the vantage point of the overall perspective.

122-123 ■ The impressive plinth, decorated with bas reliefs, supports the monolithic column dedicated to Tsar Alexander I. The striking Winter Palace is in the background.

Winter Palace Square is a vast space that combines a rectangular and a semicircular layout, paved so as to create an ample pedestrian precinct stretching from the Alexander I column, and displaying a rigorous design of regular links. The green nuances of the façade, cadenced by the double order of gilt capitals, reflect a Baroque influence and offset the warm shades of the semicircular building's yellow plaster. The single structure comprises five sections: the triumphal arch, two curving blocks, and two straight blocks, developing in a line for more than double the Winter Palace. These blocks form a harmonious sequence that contributes to highlighting the triumphal arch, which is flanked by the colonnade motif on the walls. No wonder so many tourists and visitors travel here not only to visit the collections in the Hermitage (whose current appearance is attributable to a restoration undertaken in the 1940s) but to admire the wonderful setting of the area as a whole. Today it seems impossible that a square that exudes such tranquility could have been the backdrop to the most significant events of Russian political life during the last century. But it was: it was where the 1905 uprisings began, triggered by the violent reaction of the Czar's Fusiliers to a workers' march. Only a few years later, in 1917, the October Revolution began here, too, with the invasion of the palace, the fall of the Kerensky government, and the first chapters of Soviet history.

PICCADILLY
CIRCUS

[LONDON ■ UNITED KINGDOM]

Piccadilly Circus' has always enjoyed great fame, due to the number of pubs, theaters, cinemas, and restaurants where Londoners, but above all numerous tourists, meet to relax. The shops and department stores, clubs and museums that crowd the adjoining areas are further attractions that make this one of the busiest squares in London, also because it is at the junction of several major thoroughfares: Piccadilly Street, Shaftesbury Avenue, Glasshouse Street, Haymarket, and Regent Street. Moreover, it is close to Carnaby Street, Soho, Trafalgar Square and Leicester Square. Its popularity has never waned: vehicular and pedestrian traffic is an integral part of the location's image, characterized not so much by the architecture as by the gleaming spots made up of huge neon hoardings affixed to the buildings.

Despite this frenetic image, Piccadilly Circus is the result of almost two centuries of

124-125 ■ Piccadilly Street, Shaftesbury Avenue, Glasshouse Street, Haymarket and Regent Street, all converging into Piccadilly Circus.

125 ■ A fountain commemorating the seventh Earl of Shaftesbury's philanthropy. An aluminum statue dedicated to the Angel of Christian Charity, often erroneously identified as the Greek god Eros, soars above a bronze basin.

history that began with one of the most significant urban refurbishments ever implemented by the English architect John Nash. It was he who successfully interpreted the social and decorative aspirations that Prince Regent George IV required to be expressed by transformation of city buildings made possible by the new wealth that poured into London in the wake of the industrial revolution. As early as 1811, Nash presented the sovereign with a city plan to develop the center of London, underpinned by the reacquisition of Marylebone, an area of over 200 hectares.

Nash's plan consisted of building terraces of houses and individual villas around a picturesque park, in tune with the district's rural spirit. The area was then to be connected via a vertical axis to Pall Mall (now very close to Piccadilly Circus), where the Regent lived at Carlton House. This was how Regent's Park developed, together with the various sections of Regent Street, which were connected by the introduction of two junctions, at what are now Piccadilly Circus and Oxford Circus, then known as Regent Circus South and Regent Circus North. However, by the 1880s, the opening of Shaftesbury Avenue triggered a radical change in the layout of Piccadilly Circus, erasing the round shape that Nash had designed, and accentuating its role as a road junction. Nonetheless, that had been its

LOCATION	YEAR OF CONSTRUCTION	AREA	APPLICATION	STYLE
LONDON (UNITED KINGDOM)	1819	APPROXIMATELY 28,000 SQ FEET	TRAFFIC SQUARE	STRATIFIED NEOCLASSICISM TO HISTORICISM

original role: Piccadilly Street was the ancient road that led out of London, while Haymarket was the location of the cattle market, before it was moved, in the eighteenth century, to what is now Mayfair. (Further confirmation of this history comes from the presence of one of London's many underground stations on the Bakerloo Line which opened in 1906 and was upgraded in 1928 because of a significant increase in traffic.) In short, the original architecture of Piccadilly Circus is merely a distant memory now, as the site has undergone countless refurbishments that have profoundly changed its appearance.

Today Piccadilly Circus is haphazard and inconsistent in shape because of the intersecting roads that converge there and are forced to revolve around an oblong pedestrian area. Looming above it all is the monumental fountain, set off-center at the top of Shaftesbury Avenue, commemorating the philanthropic activities of the seventh Earl of Shaftesbury, Anthony Ashley-Cooper. This 1893 bronze work comprises a hexagonal bowl set on a short flight of steps and crowned with an aluminum statue made by Alfred Gilbert, and dedicated to the Angel of Christian Charity – or, as he is mistakenly identified – the Greek god, Eros.

126-127 and 127 top ■ Piccadilly Circus, crossed daily by cars and buses, hums with activity.

127 bottom ■ Piccadilly Circus has an entrance to London's famous Tube at every corner.

Piccadilly is home to the Criterion Theatre and the London Pavillion, now called the Pepsi Trocadero, after having been completely overhauled in 2000 with funding from the Pepsi Cola company, and connected to the old Trocadero arcade. One of Europe's biggest and most important entertainment complexes, the Pepsi Trocadero is host to various edutainment installations that include a rock music museum, a James Bond adventure simulator and a Planet Hollywood franchise. The arcade is located on the northwest flank of Piccadilly Circus, on the corner of Shaftesbury Avenue and Coventry Street, and it may be said that despite the interventions to which it has been subjected, it is an example of continuity of its original function.

The Trocadero was built in 1859 as an entertainment location with a concert hall, and rebuilt in 1885, when Shaftesbury Avenue was opened. In the 1930s it became a movie theater; and in the 1980s, a shopping center. Now it has been reconverted once more and connects directly with the underground station. The Criterion Theatre on the opposite side of Piccadilly Circus, going south, was built in 1874 by Thomas Verity, using a Historicist style, and renovated in 1989. It is still in use as a theater.

There is no doubt that the heart of Milan beats in Piazza Duomo, the center of the concentric circles that characterize the city's layout. Established by a nineteenth-century urban plan designed by the engineer Ce-

sare Beruto, in 1884, and playing a significant role in the subsequent growth of this metropolis, the configuration owes its origins primarily to the demolitions that began in 1865, in the area around the Duomo, Cordusio, and La Scala, Milan's opera house. From it a system of radial streets propelled and modified the previous layout, and gave the center of the city its current configuration, and the piazza the layout designed by Giuseppe Mengoni, even though it was not realized in full.

The square's history goes back more than a thousand years and began in the fifth century, when the site now occupied by Piazza Duomo held a church that was later dedicated to Saint Tecla. In the early ninth century, behind the church, where the cathedral now stands, the Santa Maria Maggiore basilica was built, with the San Giovanni alle Fonti baptistery in between the two. The presence of two buildings of worship so close together did not create any problems: in fact, the custom arose of using them in turn, and this continued until the end of the 1450s. Santa Tecla was used in summer, because it had a front quadriporticus that increased its capacity, whilst Santa Maria Maggiore became the *hiemalis* church. The springtime swap occurred dur-

128-129 ■ The images highlights the size of the square in front of the Cathedral's marble solidity, and the triumphal archway of Mengoni's Arcade, with its cross arms and central cupola symbolizing the technical revolution implemented in architecture through the use of iron and glass.

129 ■ Giuseppe Mengoni's plan, never completely implemented, focused on the massive Cathedral, and the layout of the Arcade with its cross vault stand.

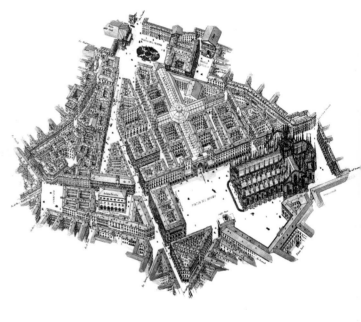

ing Easter Sunday mass. The piazza's decor was a constant concern for the various rulers, but they were fairly unsuccessful in addressing it until the ducal period: as early as 1333 Azzone Visconti issued a decree to clear the piazza (then called "dei Polli" or "Chicken Square") of its wine and roast meat stalls. Repeated efforts only made thestallholders dig in their heels, however, and it was not until 1832 that the stands crowding the square finally disappeared. Nowadays a few, controlled "stations" are back, in unobtrusive positions, selling roast chestnuts or drinks, depending on the season.

The events linked to the extension and refurbishment of the piazza are closely connected with the building of the cathedral, which began in about 1386: construction started with an east-facing apse, as was usual, and englobed the church of Santa Maria Maggiore, which was demolished within the Duomo itself as building requirements gradually imposed on it. The façade, however, was maintained until the eighteenth century, after which the road to an extensive succession of completion projects was finally open. Soon the growing sacred building found itself competing for space with the existing constructions. Apart from this, the cathedral was then found to be turned to a 45° angle on the axis of the ancient Roman grid, along which Broletto Vecchio was installed: the public building was subsequently pulled back several times as work progressed and in 1461, Santa Tecla was entirely demolished in order to make room for the Duomo and ensure it had a large parvis.

In the second half of the eighteenth century, Giuseppe Piermarini, who was appointed to remodel the building now known as Palazzo Reale (but then called Corte Ducale, as can be

LOCATION	YEAR OF CONSTRUCTION	AREA	APPLICATION	STYLE
MILAN (ITALY)	14TH-20TH CENTURY	APPROXIMATELY 193,750 SQ FEET	RELIGIOUS AND CIVIC SQUARE	STRATIFIED GOTHIC TO 1900s

seen from the map of Milan drawn in 1734 by Marc' Antonio Dal Re), ordered the north wall of the first court to be demolished and opened what is now Piazzetta di Palazzo Reale. The building's lowest wing, now called Manica Lunga, stretched westwards and met the old hamlet of Contrada dei Cappellari, so that the corner of the southern side of the Duomo's façade separated two spaces of almost the same size. In 1807 the d'Ornato Commission suggested an overhaul of the entire area, and various plans were put forward for adjustments, from one by Giuseppe Pistocchi, who intended to enclose the new piazza with regular, four-story buildings, to Carlo Amati's lavish concept of installing colonnades around the sides of the Duomo. In 1863, after the unification of Italy, the project resumed under the guidance of Giuseppe Mengoni, who not only built the famous Galleria Vittorio Emanuele II, but also decided to close the large basin with a "Loggia Reale" intended to balance this arcade, as well as a monumental Palazzo dell' Indipendenza. As it happened, only the Galleria – later the premier salon of Milan – and the porticoes on the south side of the piazza were built.

In 1886-87, the most important backdrop of the piazza neared completion: the Duomo façade. This was designed by the young Giuseppe Brentano, the winner of a competition, but his te untimely death brought work to a halt and the building retained the fusion of late 1500s and Neo-gothic lines bequeathed by the earlier work of Carlo Amati and Giuseppe Zanoja. In 1934 another competition was held for the construction of the cathedral bell tower, but

131 ■ The monument dedicated to King Vittorio Emanuele II fit perfectly into the geometrical divisions of the paving.

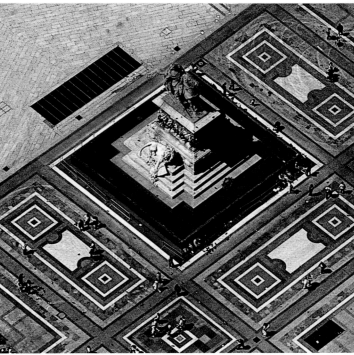

130-131 ■ The lavishly decorated pinnacles of the Duomo spires soar vertically against the square's geometrical paving stones.

nothing came of this, although the Manica Lunga was demolished to make way for Palazzo dell' Arengario, the result of a 1937 competition, won by the group comprised of Enrico A. Griffini, Pier Giulio Magistretti, Giovanni Muzio and Piero Portaluppi, and concluded in 1956.

The "ongoing piazza" continues to be the focus of architectural schemes and debates even today. It is a regular rectangle dominated by the white mass, soaring pinnacles and spires of the Duomo, which conjure up a mental picture of French Gothic constructions. To the left of the façade, which reveals the layers of its history, opens the majestic archway of the Galleria with its cross-plan and iron and glass vault, an 1800s emblem of middle-class society and the blossoming of public life. This building also plays a significant role in connecting Piazza Duomo directly to Piazza della Scala, via a roofed shopping centre. Arcaded buildings, also by Mengoni, complete the two long sides: to the north, broken by the Galleria; and to the south, concluding in the Arengario complex, comprising two twin pavilions set at the sides of Via Marconi.

In a sense, the piazza is still a work in progress: the pavilion connected to Palazzo Reale will house the Museo del Novecento [the museum of the twentieth century], when architect Italo Rota's refurbishment is complete. The piazza became a pedestrian precinct some while ago and is crossed underground by metro lines 1 and 2. Aligned with the Duomo portal stands a bronze monument dedicated to King Vittorio Emanuele II.

PIAZZA DELLA
UNITÀ D'ITALIA

[TRIESTE ■ ITALY]

Piazza Grande, or Piazza dell'Unità d'Italia, as it is now called, has been renovated many times over, and its current appearance, looking out to sea, is attributable to nineteenth-century interventions preceded by furious debate and differences of opinion between the city council and various private groups, including the insurance company Assicurazioni Generali, which played a major role. The first traces of the square, according to historians, are rooted in the city's first Palazzo Comunale (town hall) and date back to emancipation from the dominion of the bishops, in about 1252, when it became possible to begin an independent building. The chosen site was originally a Roman port, which later silted up through neglect and natural causes. The site was never abandoned and actually became the heart of the city: as time passed, the building changed shape but not scope so that even now, Palazzo Comunale and the piazza are the backdrop and setting for city life.

The piazza assumed its current size and features thanks to a second infilling, at Mandracchio, which

132-133 ■ The image shows a regular, rectangular plan whose axial structure is underscored by the design of the paving.

133 ■ The Teti statue by Giuseppe Pokorny is set at one end of the Lloyd Triestino building façade, and is balanced by the statue of Venus, sculptured by Ugo Haedti.

took place in two phases, in 1858 and 1863. The elimination of the small medieval dock resulted in the increase of available space and allowed for a total redesign of the area, which at that time consisted of a square with buildings on all four sides. About two decades of contrasting discussions and theories preceded the initiation of works, but once they got under way, they were completed quickly and involved not only the piazza and Palazzo Comunale, but also all the adjacent buildings, leading to the creation of Piazza Grande, or "Piazza dell'Unità d'Italia," as we know it today.

Throughout, two theories were considered: a single piazza, or two piazzas divided by Palazzo Comunale. Various projects in the 1850s and 1860s focused on a single great basin opening out to sea, but as late as the 1870s the municipal council had made no resolution preferring either option. In the meantime, interest grew among large private groups with regard to the opportunities that this operation would generate, while the municipal council, forced to request the involvement of such groups following difficulties in funding the project themselves, was forced to accept the demands of the investors who came to their aid. Thus in 1872, when the city fathers unveiled a plan by Giuseppe Giuliuzzi that recovered the idea of two squares separated by the town hall, a new debate raged. In the end, the idea of a single, large square overlooking the sea prevailed, and Giuseppe Bruni won the competition for a new Palazzo Comunale. His creation (completed 1873-1875) gave the square a scenographic historicist backdrop that ably interweaves Venetian Renaissance and German Mannerism nuances.

134 ■ The rich mosaic-finish wall of Palazzo della Imperial Regia Luogotenenza – later Palazzo del Governo, today the Prefecture – faces the Lloyd building; one of the eight lampposts predating the upgrading of the square, stands out against the building front.

134-135 ■ The sculpture group commemorating the Bersaglieri landing at Trieste in 1918 stands against the backdrop of the Lloyd Triestino building, today Palazzo della Regione, a typical example of 19th-century Historicist architecture.

The majority of the buildings that form the perimeter were built at the same time: Bruni realized Palazzo Modello, next to the existing Casa Stratti, which was renovated by Eugenio Geiringer; architect of the Hôtel set on the opposite side of the square, next to Palazzo Pitteri. As the century drew to a close, the final terraces emerged: the Lloyd Austro-Ungarico (later Lloyd Triestino) building, by Heinrich von Ferstel, and the Imperial Regia Luogotenenza (now the Prefecture), by Emil Artmann. Meanwhile the interred Mandracchio area became the site of a public garden.

In 1938 the Continenti Fountain was moved (and then replaced, in 1970) and no further modifications to the piazza occurred until, in 1999, the municipal authority announced a competition by invitation to upgrade Piazza Grande, Piazza Verdi, and Piazza della Borsa. In point of fact, they were a correlated system of spaces where the city's medieval quarters met the districts built under Marie Therese and Franz Josef.

The winners were Bernard Huet – a Frenchman – and the Venetian Associated Architects firm of Ceschia and Mentil, and their intent was to "reinforce the image and the identity of

LOCATION	YEAR OF CONSTRUCTION	AREA	APPLICATION	STYLE
TRIESTE (ITALY)	19TH CENTURY; 2000-2001	APPROXIMATELY 172,000 SQ FEET	CIVIC SQUARE	HISTORICISM AND CONTEMPORARY UPGRADING

each piazza, using simple means to provide downstated expression, but seeking perpetuity in keeping with the span of the city's existence: the historian Braudel's *longue durée*."

The current layout of Piazza Grande, which is a pedestrian precinct except for the seafront area, gives tangible evidence that his goal was met: the piazza's historic rectangular plan, with the short side facing the Adriatic, is reinforced by the choice of paving: gray sandstone encircled with a band of Istria stone, which enhances its unitary nature. Nonetheless, the different flooring fabric highlights the site's urban history: the sandstone slabs are set at 45°, starting at the piazza's central axis, near the city hall, and cadenced by the eight existing lampposts, while toward Mandracchio – indicating the site of the long-gone garden and the old port – the slabs are set in line and interspersed with *cabochons* of white Aurisina stone installed withelectroluminescent blue diodes. They create a carpet of light that extends from today's Prefecture to the Lloyd building's neo-Renaissance façade, not conspicuous by day, though eye-catching at night.

The square's axiality and its bond with the sea, which give it its spectacular underpinning, are deftly emphasized by the pedestrian link that slides into a shoreline stroll. A rectangular insert outlined in white stone extends between the two 1933 "flagpoles" designed by Attilio Selva underscores the city hall axis and, on the side with vehicle access, indicates the presence of pedestrians.

THEATERPLATZ

[DRESDEN ■ GERMANY]

136-137 and 136 bottom ■
The aerial views show the
proportions of the "third
Semperoper", dominating
the square's open space,
where the 19th-century
monument dedicated to
the sovereign Johann von
Sachs is erected in the
center.

Sadly, Dresden, famous as the Florence of the Elbe, for its architectural heritage, was practically razed to the ground by the bombings at the end of World War II. Such was the destruction that its most famous building, the Frauenkirche ("Church of Our Lady") was only reopened to the public in 2006, and several other historic buildings are still under restoration. Unfortunately, Theaterplatz ("theater square") the city's stunning riverbank plaza, was also seriously damaged at that time, when the *Semperoper*, or Semper Opera (after its architect, Gottfried Semper) was bombed.

This theater had been "the" symbol of Dresden's cultural and artistic life since its construction in 1841, so much so that it gave its name to the square where it was built and was undeniably its most significant feature. It was rebuilt as early as 1860, when the structure collapsed following a disastrous fire that made it necessary to reconstruct the main backdrop to the square. The citizens demanded that Semper be entrusted with this new project, and it was he who created the opera site basically as it looks today (though it was completed by son, Manfred. Given the destruction of *that* building during the Second World War, today's theater is really the *third* opera house. It was rebuilt "how it was and where it was" in 1975, three decades after the end of the War that left it a mere shell. The building is still the square's defining element and a striking memorial of city life. Today's square is also influenced by its relationship with the Zwinger, a Late Baroque

137 ■ The Semperoper entrance is surmounted by a richly-decorated exedra and crowned by a bronze sculpture group of Dionysius and Ariadne on a chariot drawn by panthers, the work of Johannes Schilling.

LOCATION	YEAR OF CONSTRUCTION	AREA	APPLICATION	STYLE
DRESDEN (GERMANY)	19TH CENTURY; 20TH-CENTURY RECONSTRUCTION	APPROXIMATELY 86,000 SQ FEET	CIVIC SQUARE	STRATIFIED BAROQUE TO 1900s

residence built in the early 1700s to designs by Matthäus D. Pöppelmann for the Elector of Saxony, Augustus the Strong.

The Zwinger was built in a C shape comprising pavilions and exterior galleries that formed an inner court with a garden opening onto the River Elbe. In 1835, when Semper was already entrusted with the construction of the theater, he thought of creating an imperial "forum" by extending the wings of the C down as far as the river. The theater was to be joined to the building by a service block; and the Gemälde Galerie, an art gallery, was to be built opposite (1839-55). However, the Diet of Saxony decided that the art gallery, also by Semper, was to be the closing element of the Zwinger, and so it became one of the chief features of the square. As a result there was no need to demolish the guards corps barracks designed by Karl Friedrich Schinkel, completed in 1830, which stood close by the Zwinger. On the other side, past Sophienstrasse, there were already the Catholic Hofkirche church apse, an eighteenth-century Baroque piece by Gaetano Chiaveri, and a castle, a residence given a Renaissance refurbishment in the sixteenth century and now largely rebuilt. Lastly, in the early twentieth

138-139 ■ Opposite the Semperoper, the apse and flank of Hofkirche, the Baroque Catholic church designed by the Italian, Gaetano Chiaveri, and the castle, a princely residence where a magnificent view can be enjoyed from its tower.

139 ■ The River Elbe flows stately at the side of the Hofkirche and the castle, against the backdrop of the Semperoper's great illuminated mass.

century, the square's privileged contact with the river was limited by a small pavilion, called the "Italienisches Dörfchen," or Italian village, commemorating the workers who built the church.

Theaterplatz, despite the many vicissitudes it suffered, nonetheless remains the heart of Dresden's cultural life, and the city has always insisted on rebuilding the square, recovering with great sacrifice the morphology devastated by the last war. Today it is an open space, with the embankment road closing it at one end and opposite it the austere façade of the neo-Renaissance art gallery, characterized by the rustic ashlar of the ground floor and a first floor decorated with Corinthian semi-columns that frame huge arched windows. The art gallery's slightly jutting central block is modeled as a triumphal arch, connecting the square with the Zwinger. In the background, the massive curving silhouette of the "third Semperoper" closes the view and deliberately conceals the new service blocks to preserve the atmosphere created for the square in the nineteenth century. Now used as a restaurant, the Italienisches Dörfchen is to the right of the theater, aligned with the bank of the Elbe, while on the edge of Sophienstrasse, opposite the village, the Neoclassical guard corps barracks, its pronaos set on Ionic columns, keeps watch on the entrance to the square. Nowadays the paving has been redesigned in a brick and gray color scheme, aligned with the square's main axes, which correspond to the position of the theater and the art gallery and delineating the center of the space,

MARIA
THERESIEN
PLATZ

[VIENNA ■ AUSTRIA]

140-141 ■ The square is set between the Art History and the Natural History Museums, and against the backdrop of the Hofstallgebäude, the trade fair center.

141 ■ The base of the monument to the Empress Marie Therese is completed by bronze statues of the generals of her Empire.

Maria Theresien Platz is found along the Burg Ring, one of the most typical areas of Vienna's Ringstrasse, the famous nineteenth-century boulevard designed to compete with the transformation of Paris conducted by famous prefect Hausmann. Maria Theresien Platz is located by the Burgtor, the castle gate erected in 1824, which is the figurative link with Helden Platz, the plaza dedicated to heroes, where the monumental Hofburg castle is located. Historically speaking, the two squares share their design, and both are moreover connected with the building of the Ringstrasse itself. The latter was initiated in 1857, when the Emperor Franz Josef issued a decree establishing what would replace the demolished medieval walls that surrounded the old center of Vienna.

"Around the *Innere Stadt* [the part of the city that lay within the demolished walls], an avenue at least 40 *toises* in length shall be built, with pedestrian and horse paths on both sides, so as to create a sort of decoration alternating monumental buildings with open spaces, to be used as gardens." This instruction taken from the imperial decree allows us to perceive the features that mold the Ringstrasse's composition, which is indeed made up of a sequence of public structures of impressive visual impact alternating with large green areas. One of the most significant is Maria Theresien Platz, which, ironically enough, is the result of a tormented design process that involved a succession of disputed competition stages and the removal of the official winner to privilege the Prussian architect Gottfried Semper.

140 bottom ■ The overall perspective of the Kaiserforum, as designed by Gottfried Semper, showing Maria Theresien Platz as it continues into Heldenplatz.

142 ■ The Empress Marie Therese depicted on her throne and set on a plinth decorated with statues 65 feet in height.

142-143 ■ The Natural History Museum designed by the architect, Semper in neo-Renaissance style, decorated with bas reliefs illustrating its function.

The area set aside for the square was in fact secondary to the construction of the history of art and natural history museums, but was above all near the Burgtor, and thus close to the Hofburg: this situation enhanced the potential and interest in the project, also because there was a need to enlarge the actual building. The first competition was held in 1867 and reserved for a clique of local architects Theophil von Hansen, Heinrich von Ferstel, Moritz Löhr and Carl von Hasenauer – all of whose designs were held to be totally unsatisfactory. One year later, a second stage of the competition was held, and Moritz Löhr was chosen, without much enthusiasm, as the winner. It was at this point that Carl von Hasenauer, wrote to Gottfried Semper, who was then at the peak of his fame, seeking an opinion outside of the jury. In 1869 the latter architect was officially appointed advisor and recommended that none of the designs be executed, pinpointing a major defect, namely was the absence of a specific individuality with respect to the bulky Hofburg and a real connection with the urban fabric.

Not long afterwards, the Emperor Franz Josef himself appointed Semper to review the project with the idea of extending the Hofburg and asking him to work with one of the architects who had taken part in the competition. Semper and von Hasenauer then designed the majestic Kaiserforum, set against the backdrop of the renovated Hofburg, and dominated by the twin blocks of the two museums. Set one opposite the other, they were sepa-

LOCATION	YEAR OF CONSTRUCTION	AREA	APPLICATION	STYLE
VIENNA (AUSTRIA)	1867; 1872-1881	APPROXIMATELY 307,000 SQ FEET	CIVIC SQUARE	HISTORICISM

rated by huge geometric flowerbeds, and used the Burgtor as an axis for their symmetry. Beyond this, across the Burg Ring, two exedras, also symmetrical and aligned with the museums, were planned to extend the Hofburg, while the old building was concealed and completed by a structure to house the imperial offices. The project was approved immediately by the Emperor but implemented very slowly and never completed, so that what one sees now is only part of the total scheme. Maria Theresien Platz thus lies between the Burg Ring and Museum Strasse, delimited by two streets and the compact volumes of the two museums, erected in Neo-renaissance style and decorated with sculptures that are intended to illustrated the contents. The central sections of the two museums are underscored by a tall cupola supported by a windowed drum and flanked by two soaring towers; they are furthermore aligned with the bronze statue of the Empress Marie Therese of Austria, which is set on a 65-foot base at the center of this eponymous square. A rectangular garden square, the Platz is today split into four identical, large flower beds and set in a scenario that embraces the Burg Ring and the Burgtor, the mass of the old Hofburg and one of the blocks designed by Semper, the exedra aligned with the art history museum. Beyond Museum Strasse, the backdrop to the garden square is formed by the exhibition center, installed in the imperial stables built in 1723-27 by Fischer von Erlach.

HŐSÖK TERE

[BUDAPEST ■ HUNGARY]

In 1992 Budapest's lovely Hősök Tere (Heroes' Square) gained protection for posterity via its inclusion on UNESCO's list of World Heritage Sites, thanks to the extension of a previous act undertaken to protect the banks of the Danube and the Buda Castle quarter. This protection extends as far up as the stunning backdrop provided by Andrassy útja, the avenue that leads to the square.

For various reasons Hősök Tere is the most complete expression of the nation's history, narrated as it is through its outstanding sculptures, from the conquest of Hungary by the great Árpád and his Magyars And on down through the centuries. Leaders, sovereigns, and statesmen of later eras are depicted by statues that breathe life into the hemicycles that compose the monument. Several of the statues of Hapsburg dynasty monarchs were removed in the 1950s, when the Soviet Union influenced decision-making in Hungary and other Eastern Bloc countries, but they have now been restored.

Heroes Square was conceived in 1896 by architect Albert Schickedanz and sculptor György Zala to complete Andrassy útja, as well as to celebrate the 1000th anniversary

144-145 ■ A trabeated exedra colonnade forms the celebratory monument for the 1000th anniversary of the conquest of Hungary.

145 ■ The allegories of War and Peace decorate the central tips of the Millennium Emlékmű monument's colonnade.

of the Magyar conquest of Hungary. It was officially inaugurated in 1929. The premise for this commemorative scheme originated in the events of 1873, when the cities of Buda and Pest were united, with the ensuing constitution of a real capital for the nation and subsequent urban growth. Budapest soon expanded quickly, especially around several main streets, following a plan prepared by a special commission of public works, modeled on London's Metropolitan Board of Works.

Andrassy útja was one of the chief radials reaching beyond the core of the old city, which was thus connected to Városliget, the civic park, and further integrated by the installation of a subway (completed 1896) that was the first in continental Europe. To mark the millennium anniversary celebrations, which included a great art and trade expo, it was decided that a monumental square, Hősök Tere, would be built at the end of Andrassy útja, and that the park behind it would be extended, endowing it with new structures. The Széchenyi spa facilities, the Közlekdési transport museum, and the Vajahunyad Vára castle, which comprise 21 copies of different parts of historical Hungarian buildings, were thus erected along the park avenues.

Heroes' Square was designed as a round open space, decorated with fountains and flowerbeds, and
containing an impressive 120-foot Corinthian column set on a plinth, flanked by two hemicycle wings, and
comprising a sequence of trabeated columns interposed with sculp-
tures. The square was completed by two fundamental buildings for
the kind of capital Budapest had become and for the occasion to be
celebrated: firstly Albert Schickedanz's Műcsarnok, the art gallery
for touring exhibits, which was finished in 1895, and secondly the Szép-
művészeti Múzeum, or Fine Arts Museum, which opened in 1906. It too
was built by Schickedanz, with the assistance of Fülöp Herzog.

Today's Hősök Tere has retained its circular plan but has been
paved in a geometrical motif that divides the space between the Millennium Monument, the Fine Arts Museum, and the Art Gallery. Both
of the latter buildings have classically-inspired facades that were designed to stand facing one another: the museum's front is a sequence of three pavilions, each closed by a neo-Classical Corinthian
pronaos and connected by colonnades, whereas the gallery is deco-

146-147 ■ The equestrian
statues of Árpád and the
chiefs of the Magyar tribes
who conquered Hungary
encircle the base of the
soaring Corinthian column
set between the monument's
two hemicycles.

LOCATION	YEAR OF CONSTRUCTION	AREA	APPLICATION	STYLE
BUDAPEST (HUNGARY)	1896-1906	APPROXIMATELY 172,000 SQ FEET	CIVIC SQUARE	HISTORICISM

rated by a single, impressive Corinthian pronaos annexed to a simple parallelepiped block. Between them stands the Millennium Monument, a soaring Corinthian column that holds a bronze statue of the Archangel Gabriel with the crown of St. Stephen, its base is encircled by equestrian statues of Árpád and the chiefs of the Magyar tribes. The column is the barycenter for the two hemicycles decorated with sculptures of Hungarian sovereigns, statesmen, and heroes, while at each end there are allegories of Work and Wellbeing, Honesty and Glory, with Peace and War in the center. Apart from this monument there is also that of the Unknown Soldier.

Hősök Tere holds an important place in national memory and has been the theater of several significant events in Hungarian history: in 1989, more than three decades after his death, Imre Nagy was given a state funeral here, and in 1991 Pope John Paul II celebrated a solemn mass for 200,000 faithful.

PLAZA DE
MAYO

[BUENOS AIRES ■ ARGENTINA]

There is no doubt that the architectural center of Buenos Aires is Plaza de Mayo, a large urban space created by uniting two older neighboring squares. Plaza de Mayo is where the most important public buildings now stand; moreover, it has been the site of the country's most momentous political and religious events since the nineteenth century.

As it is now laid out, Plaza de Mayo emerged in 1884, the year when the building separating Plaza de la Victoria from Plaza del Fuerte was demolished to unite the two sites. The name of the resulting new square commemorates the revolution of May 1810, which brought independence from Spain six years later, in 1816. Nowadays the site is sufficiently important for it to be known as a "microcentro porteño." Three major thoroughfares – Diagonal Sur (or Presidente Julio Argentino Roca), Diagonal Norte (or Presidente Roque Sáenz Peña), and Avenida de Mayo – meet here; and it is also around this square that the most important monuments stand.

Buenos Aires has a regular checkerboard layout, where each checker, or "manzananas," is about 32,500 sq ft, and where the wide streets intersect at right angles. Plaza de Mayo

 148-149 ■ The aerial view shows the axial paving design applied to the square, drawing attention to the presence of the Casa Rosada.

148 bottom ■ Tourists and residents alike cross the plaza around the "pyramid", or relax near the tree-lined flowerbeds skirting the construction.

150 top ■ The small
obelisk set at the center
of the square is called
the "pyramid" and was
erected to commemorate
the May 18 revolution.

150-151 ■ The Casa Rosada, with its distinctive pink
cladding, is the seat of the Republic of Argentina's
executive powers.

150 bottom ■ The mock-Classical pronaos of the
Metropolitan Cathedral flanks the square with
its stately Corinthian colonnade.

occupies two manzananas, so has an area of 65,000 sq ft, stretching from west to east for
about 650 feet, and from north to south for about 325 feet. There are several undergound
stations beneath the plaza, connecting it quickly to various points in the city, which has over
14,000,000 inhabitants if the suburbs are included. Avenida de Mayo, coming from the west,
leads into the square precisely opposite the Casa Rosada, thus offering a vista of the seat
of federal government in all its glory. The west side of the plaza houses the Cabildo, the
building that is the symbol of the city's colonial past. Rebuilt on a smaller scale (in compari-
son to the 1764 original) it is now the home of the National History Museum.

Important buildings in the square include the Metropolitan Cathedral, built on the
spot where the Iglesia Mayor, or "great church" stood in 1593. Since then the place of worship has been refurbished on various occasions, as previous constructions deteriorated,
and this has changed its appearance extensively. The latest of these modifications was
the one that had the greatest impact and gave it the neoclassical plan it now has; it took

LOCATION	YEAR OF CONSTRUCTION	AREA	APPLICATION	STYLE
BUENOS AIRES (ARGENTINA)	1884	212,190 SQ FEET	RELIGIOUS AND CIVIC SQUARE	HISTORICISM

place from 1860 to 1863, at the hands of Joseph Dubourdieu, and the visitor will be astonished by the contrast between his imprint on the building: a colonial Spanish-style interior, and an exterior marked by rigorous linearity. Also worthy of note are Palacio de Gobierno de la Ciudad de Buenos Aires, the seat of Buenos Aires' municipal government, built from 1891 to 1902, and the Old National Congress building that now houses the National Academy of History.

At the center of the square is the so-called Pirámide de Mayo, an obelisk commemorating the bloody revolution of May 1810, holding a symbol of the Republic. The square has been the theater of impressive rallies that have marked Argentinian civic life right up to the present day: on 17 October 1945 a union demonstration ensured the release of Juan Domingo Perón, who became national president, and this is where the crowds of *descamisados* met to acclaim Evita Perón. In the Seventies the "Madres de Plaza de Mayo" began to assemble here, silently protesting the disappearance of relatives and loved ones who had disappeared into the prisons and graveyards of the repressive military regime then in power. The latest events in the plaza date back to 2001, when protesters were attacked and dispersed by the police after a popular revolt triggered by the terrible economic crisis that risked disaster for the country.

TIMES
SQUARE

[NEW YORK ■ USA]

152 ■ Times Square's compacted space is hemmed in by towering skyscrapers.

152-153 ■ Taxis darting frenetically underscore the vitality of Times Square, ablaze with its iconic garish colored neon lights.

Located at the junction of Broadway, 42nd Street, and 7th Avenue, the beating heart of New York City's theater and entertainment district, Times Square is one of the most famous crossroads in the world,. As with its famous British counterpart, London's Piccadilly Circus, thousands of vehicles – and tens of thousands of pedestrians – pass through it every day, rushing under (or stopping to gawk up at) the enormous neon billboards that cover many of the buildings around the square, which turn it into one of the city's most recognizable icons as the sun goes down. The northern part of Times Square, although not a separate physical entity, is dedicated to Francio Duffy, the Catholic chaplain of the unit of Irish soldiers who fought in France during World War I and who was the parish priest of a neighboring church. At the end of the nineteenth century the area was known as Longacre Square and was populated mainly by horse traders and blacksmiths, but in just a few years it changed radically and the site turned into the keystone of the Theater District. The first two playhouses – the Victory and the Republic – were built in 1899, and these were followed

by numerous others, spread throughout Broadway and 42nd Street, like the New Amsterdam, which opened in 1903. A year later a tower block was built, subsequently to give its name to the crossroads: designed by architects Cyrus L.W. Eidlitz and James C. MacKenzie, it became the premises of the famous daily *The New York Times*, whose move there in 1904 was decided by the editor Adolph S. Ochs. Not long after a subway station was also opened there and the site officially became Times Square, bringing on its heyday. Billboards, posters and neon signs appeared on the façades, advertising theater shows, promoting products, or announcing news of import to passersby. A neon sign at the foot of the newspaper's old offices, dating to 1928, when it was installed to inform the public that H. C. Hoover had won the presidential elections, is still there. In the Twenties, the area became the "Great White Way" of Broadway, since the entire quarter had been electrified and attracted throngs for whom it exemplified a technological marvel or wonderland. In 1927 the Paramount Building was built to designs by the architects Rapp & Rapp. The headquarters of Paramount Pictures and the Paramount Theater, seating over 3,000, made the location even more famous, drawing bigger crowds than ever.

The Great Depression, in 1929, stopped the golden age in its tracks and a slow but sure decline began, culminating in the onset of sex shops and hardcore movie theaters. The situation deteriorated consistently until the 1990s, when Mayor Rudolph Giuliani initiated a series of schemes to restore the area and the Times Square Business Improvement District was founded. This organization's members included the municipal council, businesses and civic associations, and was dedicated to refurbishment of the old playhouses, movie theaters and concert halls in an endeavor to recover the quarter's original layout and clientele.

Today, a revitalized and "family-friendly" Times Square is once again the focal point of the Theater District, glittering with bright lights and squeezed on all sides by the high-rise blocks around it: the Times Tower, the old New York Times offices, still soars 26 floors up to evoke the history of the place, although in 1966 it was stripped of its brick cladding in favor of marble slabs that have altered its architectural spirit. The massive Paramount Building has also been modified extensively: its auditorium has gone, replaced by offices, but the top of the building outside is identical, with 14 huge steps sloping up towards the roof and topped by a globe. Each December 31, the Square hosts its wildly popular New Year's festivities, as it has done since 1904, when The New York Times opened its new head offices: a ball slides down a pole, and crowds cheer in the new year.

154 ■ **Times Square is at the fork of Broadway, 42nd Street and 7th Avenue: it is the heart of the entertainment district, teeming with playhouses and movie theaters.**

154-155 ■ **Times Square's garish night-time illumination is created by electric billboards that were introduced as early as the turn of the 20th century, and established the plaza's image from the very start.**

155 bottom ■ Restaurants, cinemas and billboards plaster their logos across the famous square, contributing to its international fame, beckoning tourists and residents alike to their premises.

LOCATION	YEAR OF CONSTRUCTION	AREA	APPLICATION	STYLE
NEW YORK (USA)	EARLY 20TH CENTURY	APPROXIMATELY 33,000 SQ FEET	TRAFFIC SQUARE	STRATIFIED EARLY 1900s TO CONTEMPORARY

PLAZAS, from 1900 to the PRESENT

As can be seen in the evolution of principles adopted by CIAM – the International Congresses for Modern Architecture – and their suspension in 1959, the second half of the 1900s leaned towards deeply modified scenarios of contemplation,

proposing the redefinition of the urban structure. The search for a universal rational order as hoped for by the major players of early Modernity, in the immediate post-WWII period, was replaced by a more open-minded and flexible attitude, heeding the unique traits of locations and transformations in social fabric. Thus there were no more plans for standardized towns designed with distinct functional areas, but instead urban centers that were to inherit the legacy of historical stratifications that might add new and different functions to the wealth and complexity of tradition.

The square thus returned to its role as a truly significant element, especially in the case of re-establishing ancient civic values: the construction of Capitol Square in Chandigarh, the new capital of the Punjab, is the most obvious example. Le Corbusier in person committed to the design of the entire city, from 1951 to 1965, applying the principles of the Charter of Athens, but in vesting them with attention to environmental conditions and local

culture. This Indian country's main government buildings converse with the Himalayan peaks from the vast Capitol platform: Parliament, High Court and Secretariat, with their plastic forms and rugged *béton brut* cladding, are set wide apart, arranged to express institutional hierarchies. The mighty physical presence of the complex influenced the forms preferred by countless architects, including Kallmann, McKinnel and Knowles, who used raw concrete for Boston's City Hall Plaza. The project is linked to the United States' urban renewal programs of the 1960s, which were often guided by a speculative spirit, redesigning entire urban districts, and using as governing elements the installation of public spaces where the population could identify itself. Nathan Phillips Square, in Toronto, on the other hand, , is the expression of an architecture who paid homage to the Modern Movement, crystallizing it in the International Style, and leaving a successful example of an intent to merge the square's social role as a meeting place with its civic function. Pools of water, sculptures and

plazas, from 1900 to the present

From top to bottom ■ Nathan Phillips Square, Toronto; Plateau Beaubourg, Paris; plaza system, Gibellina; Place de la Maison Carrée, Nîmes; Pershing Square, Los Angeles; Schouwburgplein, Rotterdam; Esplanade de la Défense, Paris; Potsdamer Platz, Berlin.

gardens make it a very livable communal site, seeking to renew urban socialization and, at the same time, the expression of a municipal authority attentive to the needs of its citizens.

Moreover, in the 1960s, youth counterculture introduced an element of fun to squares and streets, which became places of entertainment, open for "deinstitutionalized" music and theater. The Plateau in front of Paris's grand Beaubourg created by Piano and Rogers in the 1970s, exemplifies this trend of mediating between academic "museum culture" and the living culture of a people , while retaining its locus in an ancient urban heart.

In the subsequent decade, urban planning absorbed the influence of existing cultural developments and leaned to the refurbishment of run-down and peripheral areas, as was the case in Barcelona, where the municipality began with single projects and promoted the transformation of the entire urban fabric. Here there was a parallel and fundamental decision to restore a pedestrian role to historical squares, often downgraded to parking lots: they were furnished to encourage people to linger to enjoy staged events, or they were beautified with flowerbeds and lawns to make them into garden squares, like Rotterdam's Schouwburgplein, or Pershing Square in Los Angeles. So even today, squares continue to provide a vital role: they allow the public expression of social interaction that keeps the communal spirit and the civil and social values of even the largest city alive.

158-159 ■ The aerial view underscores the sheer size of the square, with the Front Gate to the south and the Gate of Heavenly Peace to the north, closing off the Forbidden City.

159 bottom ■ Observing the square from the Gate of Heavenly Peace, it is possible to see first the Monument to the People's Heroes and then Mao Zedong's mausoleum.

Tian'anmen Square is a recent construction and the result of the post-1949 gutting of the Tartar City following leader Mao Zedong's ascent to power. The name of the square, on the other hand, is laden with history and means "Gate of Heavenly Peace," after the name of the gate that separates it from the Forbidden City, to the north. Through the 1950s and into the 1960s, Beijing was extensively modified, and little regard was given to testimonies of the past. As a consequence, the walls of the urban areas known, respectively, as the Tartar City and the Chinese City, as well as almost all of the monumental gates, were lost, with only the Qianmen (Front Gate) and part of the Deshengmen (Victory of the Virtues Gate) surviving. Not even the buildings housing the offices of the imperial ministry, which had been concentrated in the area now occupied by the square, were spared. But elements of the Gate of Heavenly Peace, built in 1417 and renovated in 1651, did survive, and it has since become the icon of Tian'anmen Square, which covers the area outside of the Forbidden City previously given over to the buildings used to administer the Chinese Empire.

During the Boxer Rebellion (1899-1900), the area was so seriously damaged that a decision was made not to rebuild it, but to leave it as an open space: this was the embryo of Tian'anmen Square. Later, from 1949 onwards, it was extended to reach its current size: an endless flat expanse between the two surviving gates: the Tian'anmen and the Qianmen. Despite being the fulcrum of city life – it has been the venue of the most significant events since 1949 – it is not the city center from a geometrical standpoint. Beijing developed in two almost identical sections, along the north-south main traffic axis, and the square is set slightly to the east of this thoroughfare. This fact has not prevented the square from becoming the preferred site of public and political occurrences. On 1 October 1949, President Mao Zedong stood here as he proclaimed the birth of the People's Republic of China; and during the Cultural Revolution, the square was trampled by mass rallies of thousands waving Mao's "little red book". In 1976 it was the place where protests were voiced after the death of Zhou Enlai; and in the summer of 1989, it became synonymous with governmental repression, when hundreds of demonstrating students were slaughtered by tanks and guns.

TIAN'ANMEN

SQUARE

[BEIJING ■ CHINA]

In daily life the massive plaza is a pacific meeting place serving Beijing's citizens and the countless tourists who flock there each day, walking around it to visit the monuments that it hosts. In the center rises the monument to the People's Heroes, inaugurated on May 1, 1958. Comprised of a 125-foot granite obelisk that rests on two marble slabs, it is lavishly decorated and carved with commemorative wording on the sides.

The west side of the square is occupied by the Great Hall of the People, the main venue for the Chinese government's "high society" events, and consequently encompassing a 10,000-seat auditorium and a massive banquet hall. It is also the location of legislative offices, and some thirty 30 of its three hundred rooms are dedicated to the various provinces of China. It is one of the biggest constructions erected here and was completed in 1959, the same year Tian'anmen Square itself was finished. The building on the east side, however, already existed – it is the Museum of Chinese History, which opened in 1926 and was extended after 1949.

The last of the huge Tian'anmen Square buildings dates back to 1976 and is the mausoleum for the embalmed body of President Mao, which rests in a glass casket. It was built in just nine months, after the death of the "Great Helmsman," and runs 850 feet from north to south and 720 feet from east to west. It is surrounded by a tree-lined green area, with pines that cover a surface of about 650,000 square feet, whereas the entire area of this complex is over 16,250,000 square feet. It is precisely the immense size of Tian'anmen Square that makes it seem so infinite to Europeans, and barely suited to typical socialization; but in reality, together with its monuments, it is a fitting expression of the vastness of the country that conceived and realized it.

160-161 ■ The monumental mausoleum, housing the remains of Mao Zedong, is preceded by two groups of sculptures decorating the entrance.

160 bottom ■ Tian'anmen, that is to say the Gate of Heavenly Peace, which give the square its name, is connected to it by five pedestrian walkways.

161 bottom left ■ The Monument to the People's Heroes is a 125-foot granite obelisk, inaugurated 1 May 1958.

161 bottom right ■ Part of the building that houses the Museum of Chinese History is dedicated to the history of the Revolution. The exhibition traces the events from 1840 to the present day, particularly the growth of the Chinese Communist Party and the revolutionary movement.

LOCATION	YEAR OF CONSTRUCTION	AREA	APPLICATION	STYLE
BEIJING (CHINA)	1949-1959	4,736,120 SQ FEET	CIVIC SQUARE	SOCIALIST REALISM

162 ■ "Os Candangos" depicts the workers whose toil created the new city of Brasilia, framed by the Supreme Court of Justice.

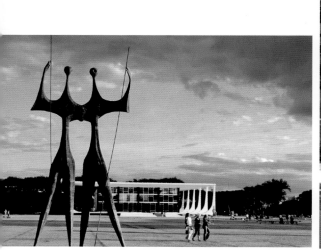

PRAÇA DOS
TRÊS PODERES

[BRASILIA ■ BRAZIL]

Praça dos Três Poderes ("Three Powers Square") is the political and administrative heart of Brasilia, the new capital city of Brazil, whose design was commissioned in September 1956 by a very determined President Juscelino Kubitschek. The urban plan was entrusted to architect Oscar Niemeyer, who accepted only the supervision of the work group and study of the city's residential and representative buildings, and suggested a competition be held to design the plan.

With its monumental representative buildings, the sqaure is set at the center of a cross conceived by Lucio Costa's "Pilot Plan" – Costa being the winner of the competition suggested by Niemeyer, whose design is an application of the principles of the modern city as stated by the Charter of Athens. Often compared to an aircraft landed on the terrain, the layout has its "pilot's cabin" in Three Powers Square, sliced by the so-called Monumental Axis. This is the city's chief axis and stretches into infinity, in a symbolic journey to the region's remotest areas, embodying the intention, manifest since the colonial era, of penetrating the heart of Brazilian territory. There is also the suggestion of reaching out towards a future dense with opportunity and the desire to express a common social program, which finds its expression in the curving, prismatic solids that compose Three Powers Square.

162-163 ■ The vast square opening out at the end of the city's monumental axis, encompassed by the buildings of the Supreme Court (left), Palácio do Planalto (right), Congress (center) and the Panteão da Pátria (below).

Before the Brasilia project in the 1930s, Costa and Niemeyer, who were both fascinated by the teachings of Le Corbusier, had already worked together to promote the introduction of Modern Movement in Brazil. Nonetheless, the principles of Modernism were quickly revamped by Niemeyer in light of his tropical background. As he later explained, "I'm not attracted by right angles." Nor by a straight line, created by human beings, and which is hard and inflexible. I am attracted, however, by the sensual, free stroke. The curve that I find in the mountains of my homeland, in the sinuous course of a river, the clouds in the sky and the body of the woman I love." Hence the conception of Three Powers Square as a set of molded "pure" forms glimpsed at the end of the impressive Esplanada dos Ministérios and animating the view behind the Brazilian Congress by ending one and opening the other.

The square has a rectangular plan and lies horizontally to the vast green Esplanada, which is the view from the glass prisms set into the ministerial offices; there are roads on two sides and gardens have been created on the other two sides.

Three Powers Square is named for the functions performed in the buildings located there: Congress, Planalto, and the Supreme Court, respectively the seats of legislative, executive and the judiciary powers. The Palácio do Planalto and the Supreme Court are set at the extremities of the square, along the short sides of the rectangular plan, and are equidistant from the Palace of Congress, with which they form an ideal equilateral triangle that symbolizes their equal importance in the life of the Republic.

164 ■ The Supreme Court of Justice comprises a glass-sided casket in a framework of streamlined pilasters with tapered tips.

164-165 ■ The Palace of Congress is distinguished by two different roofs, one for each Chamber: concave for the Senate and convex for the Deputies.

165 bottom left ■ The bust of Tiradentes, set against the backdrop of the Panteão da Pátria, the last building designed by Niemeyer for the square, in 1985.

Opposite Congress is the entrance to the Espaço Lucio Costa, dedicated to Brasilia's *maquette* and installed beneath the square; and also the Panteão da Pátria, designed by Niemeyer in 1985 and dedicated to Tancredo Neves, former president of Brazil. The square therefore comprises a vast open space surrounded by sculpture-buildings, each separate from the other but connected by a system of interrelated volumes, green spaces, and pools of water. The Palace of Congress is actually separated from the square both by a link road between the two avenues that flank the Esplanada dos Ministérios in parallel, and by the huge pool of water reflecting the tall twin towers of the Secretariat. The towers rise behind Congress' reinforced concrete slab and soar between the two Chambers, highlighted by two different domes, one concave, for the Senate, and the other convex, for the Chamber of Deputies. The roof platform is accessible and is reached by a sloping ramp similar to those connecting the government buildings to ground level. The Congress was designed to express, as Niemeyer himself said, "a character of great monumentality, with simplification of its elements and the application of pure, geometrical forms."

This intention also filters through to the other buildings that face out onto Three Powers Square, subverting several canons of functionalism, as in both Palácio do Planalto and in the

LOCATION	YEAR OF CONSTRUCTION	AREA	APPLICATION	PROJECT
BRASILIA (BRAZIL)	1957-1959 1985-1986	APPROXIMATELY 420,000 SQ FEET	CIVIC SQUARE	OSCAR NIEMEYER

Supreme Court building, in which the architect introduced extremely fine-pointed pilasters to make the structures look as if they are almost detached from the ground of the square. They resemble glass caskets suspended inside a cage finished in white marble, which narrows at the points where it touches the ground and the roof, while curving on contact with the glass case it holds.

From the center of the square a sequence of harmonious lines is visible, changing as the visitor's standpoint varies. This is completed by three works of art closely related to the buildings where they are installed: in front of Planalto is a statue by Bruno Giorni entitled *Os Candangos* – the workers who actually built Brasilia; opposite the Supreme Court there is Alfredo Ceschiatti's *Justice*; lastly, Niemeyer's *Pombal*. Last of all is the Pantheon, composed of two white spreading wings, in reinforced concrete – the material that enabled the sculpted configuration of the entire square.

 165 bottom right ▪ **A pool of water and a curving footbridge connect Three Powers Square with the Palácio do Planalto, also set on pointed pilasters.**

166 top ■ Perspective sketch of the City Hall, showing the two vertical blades that make up the building, set around the central nucleus of the Council Chamber.

166 bottom ■ The aerial view shows the City Hall in relation to the square, which symbolizes its connection to the community, thanks to facilities for the public, like the water feature.

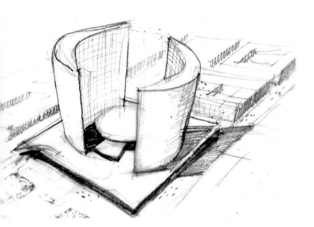

NATHAN PHILLIPS
SQUARE

[TORONTO ■ CANADA]

Nathan Phillips Square was designed by Finnish architect Viljo Revell to complete Toronto's new City Hall. Just thirty years after its construction, in 1991, the building was listed by the Ontario Heritage Act, a noteworthy recognition of status for such a recent project. The square is the result of one of the city's most successful competitions, which was passionately supported by the mayor, Nathan Phillips, and to whom it was subsequently dedicated.

The competition was held in 1957 and was presided over by an international panel which judged over 500 designs entered from 42 different countries across the globe. The commission was awarded to Finnish architect Revell, who had been involved in the results of the International Style since post-World War II.

His design of a new City Hall in a square whose role was to represent but also to provide an area for recreation was highly regarded by Mayor Phillips, who announced it to be a work of great scope, well suited to the requirements of his community.

The old municipal headquarters, a nineteenth-century building, is set next to the square and survives as a testimony of an earlier past.

166-167 ■ **An aerial view of the City Hall showing the two curving blocks of different heights, set around the Council Chamber, dominating the square dedicated to Mayor Nathan Phillips: green areas, sculptures and fountains decorate the public area, bordered by a marquise.**

LOCATION	YEAR OF CONSTRUCTION	AREA	APPLICATION	PROJECT
TORONTO (CANADA)	1957; 1961-1965	APPROXIMATELY 323,000 SQ FEET	CIVIC SQUARE	VILJO REVELL WITH JOHN PARKIN ASSOCIATES

168 bottom ■ Nathan Phillips Square is currently at the heart of a competition whose scope is to upgrade its layout, mainly by refurbishing neighbouring areas, underused since realization of the original design.

168-169 ■ Across the rectangular stretch of water that opens at one end of the square, the three "Freedom Arches", silhouetted against the old City Hall, a massive stone building completed in 1899 and designated a National Historic Site in 1989.

A large, rectangular plot, bordered by the main arteries Queen Street West and Bay Street, was at the basis of the intervention, which installed an enormous underground car park to be used by staff and visitors.

A raised pathway encircles three sides of the area, delimiting the square and connecting it to City Hall's council chamber via a ramp, between two curved towers raised on a platform. The biggest part of the plot has a garden and is installed with works of art, fountains, and a large pool of water that is intended to reflect the building's curving surfaces, blending Aalto's teachings with the cement and large windows so typical of International Modernism. The reflecting pool is shallow and was specially designed to mirror the building during fine weather; during winter, when the climate and a special refrigeration unit ensure it freezes over, it is used as a skating rink.

The square is animated by waterworks and crossed overhead by three fine cement arches known since 1989 as the "Freedom Arches," a reference to a fragment of the Berlin Wall that was set into the base of the center structure. Consequently the basin is one of the square's major attractions, always accessible to citizens and visitors. In 1984, for the 150th anniversary of the foundation of Toronto, the square underscored its role as a popular meeting place, as well as avenue for public events, performances, concerts and exhibitions, by the official inauguration of its Peace Garden, a new green space enhanced with works of art that symbolize peace.

Not far from the entrance to City Hall is an abstract sculpture, *Three-Way Piece No. 2* by Henry Moore, the British sculptor and close friend of Revell, who suggested the commission, which was accepted notwithstanding the expense. The bronze opus, which the citizens call "The Archer," stands out on the scenario that supports the two semicircular towers of different heights, with the convex section and the short sides completely covered in cement panels, a single glass panel opening in the concave part. The ovoid council chamber, resting a single hollow pilaster, rises out of the foundations and crosses the base of the building; seen from above, the layout of the complex resembles an eye staring out from its eyelids, a metaphor for the government managing and protecting the city around it.

170 The preliminary study shows a perspective of the City Hall, with the plan and the "Toronto City Hall" inscription.

170-171 ■ With the complicity of night-time lighting, the City Hall's rounded blocks appear almost suspended over the foundation slab, supported by slim pillars.

 171 bottom ■ In winter the pool becomes a handy ice rink, making Nathan Phillips Square lively at all times of day and night.

CITY HALL
PLAZA

[BOSTON ■ USA]

172-173 ■ The aerial view highlights how the snow-covered plaza slopes down against a backdrop showing the massive bulk of the City Hall and the Atlantic Ocean.

173 ■ The vertical and horizontal sections of the City Hall underscore the complexity of its structure in relation to the square's height differences, expressed in a series of terraces that mimic the downward slope as they hug the building.

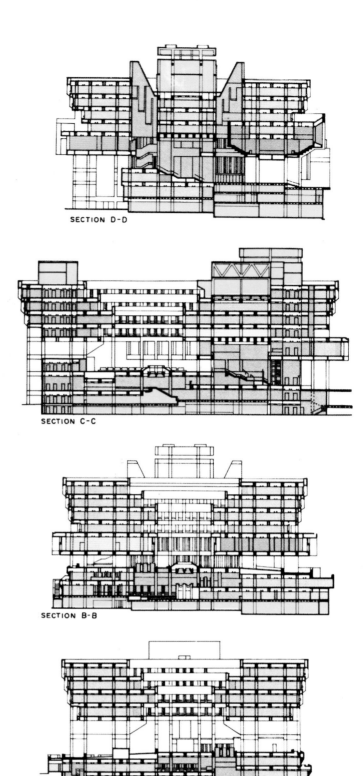

SECTION D-D

SECTION C-C

SECTION B-B

SECTION A-A

Boston's new City Hall and the square where it stands are the result of a national competition held in 1961, won by Gerhard M. Kallmann, Noel M. McKinnel and Edward F. Knowles, who effectively became the firm of architects now known as Kallmann, McKinnel, and Wood. Critics defined the complex as one of the best in America, and it won several awards. It was one outcome of the Government Center Urban Renewal Plan, whose chief devisers were the architects leo M. Pei and Henry N. Cobb.

When Boston Redevelopment Authority started its urban refurbishment scheme in 1961, it took on mainly the unified relocation of federal, state, and municipal offices in the degraded Scollay Square neighborhood, involving about 850,000 sq ft (260,000 sqm). With the exception of a handful of historical buildings, the scheme required the demolition of existing fabric and the development of services, trade, and incoming structures, as well as improvement of road connections. The heart of the concept, which laid down precise indications for height, volume, open spaces, and urban ratios, was the new plaza at City Hall. It was these planning criteria that were used as guidelines for the competition won by Kallmann, McKinnel, and Knowles; and their shaped the city's icon of

LOCATION	YEAR OF CONSTRUCTION	AREA	APPLICATION	PROJECT
BOSTON (USA)	1962-1968	APPROXIMATELY 513,000 SQ FEET	CIVIC SQUARE	GERHARD M. KALMANN, NOEL M. MCKINNEL, EDWARD F. KNOWLES

public administration in an expression both of the liberality and also of the authority of Boston's governing organs.

The great, irregularly outlined square is bordered by roads and dominated by City Hall, which stands as its fulcrum and simultaneously indicates the two main accesses, standing apart from other buildings. City Hall is actually flanked by the John F. Kennedy Federal Office Building (designed by The Architects Collaborative and Samuel Glaser Associates) and by One Center Plaza (designed by Welton Beckett and Associates), both arranged freely to form a backdrop. One Center Plaza pays homage to Boston's historic Sears Crescent, mimicking its curving evolution and providing a suitable background for City Hall. The John F. Kennedy Federal Office Building, on the other hand, defines the right side of the plaza, with its horizontal structure, finished in prefab concrete panels and offsetting the two tall towers behind it. The large open space between these buildings is used for political debate and performing arts, valorized by the presence of a small cavea.

The square is fully paved in brick and molded to the natural slope of the terrain

174-175 ■ The City Hall, focal point of the vast square, is surrounded by numerous buildings of various heights, all government offices.

175 ■ City Hall Plaza is often used for public events and performances that attract huge crowds of participants.

thanks to a series of terraces and tiers, delimited by natural white stone steps. The slope of the ramps embraces the underground part of City Hall, which has a brick-faced foundation underpinning the main body of the building in unfinished cement, an obvious reference to the *béton brut* used by Le Corbusier in his final architectures. In fact, the building is specifically inspired by the Swiss architect's design for the Convent of La Tourette, near Lyon: the *pilotis* that become supporting dividers and the *brise-soleils* that are transformed into projections to shield openings are all a homage to the great man.

City Hall features a combination of site-cast pre-stressed reinforced concrete and masonry, interwoven to suggest the building's three different functions. The lower area houses services for the public, as it is easier to access from the road, and is connected to the plaza by wide staircases; the central section is for representative functions like the mayor's office and the council chamber; and the administrative offices are to be found on the upper levels. Cement and brick unify, materially, the square's composition and the significant architectural installations looking out onto it.

PLATEAU
BEAUBOURG

[PARIS ■ FRANCE]

Place George Pompidou lies at the feet of the Centre Pompidou, the phantasmagorical museum complex designed by the youthful Renzo Piano and Richard Rogers in 1971. The open space is closely linked to the museum and dedicated to the French president who inspired it by promoted the idea of a flexible cultural center dedicated to creating and exhibiting modern art, and to theater, music, cinema, and literature. Situated in the heart of Paris, in an area vacated by the demolition of Les Halles, it was built after Piano and Rogers, won an international design competition. Both men were only 30 at the time.

Colorful, irreverent Beaubourg, as the building is usually known, expressesthe rejection of an obsolete institutional culture in favor of its total renewal, achieved by rendering it accessible to the general public. Viewed from such a premise, Plateau Beaubourg becomes a decisive element, fundamental for the museum complex and for the cultural ideal it upholds. It is almost as if Beaubourg had landed in Paris from another planet and provided the basic "hardware" to activate the era's cultural "software" of performances, art created with bodies and exhibited right on the street – or inspired by it. The earliest plans put forward by the designers described an Archigram Instant City – in other words, the prototype of a digital world *in fieri* allowing the interaction of the museum with the surrounding urban quarter.

176 ■ The museum's urban machine, flanked by the Atelier Brancusi, dominates the Plateau, which serves as an open-air lobby and is connected to the IRCAM square.

176-177 ■ The museum is accessed by escalators that gently rise away from the crowded vitality of the square and reach a point that offers a marvelous view of all Paris.

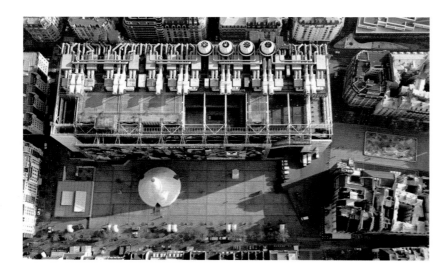

LOCATION	YEAR OF CONSTRUCTION	AREA	APPLICATION	PROJECT
PARIS (FRANCE)	1971-1977	APPROXIMATELY 32,000 SQ FEET	CIVIC SQUARE	STUDIO PIANO & ROGERS ARCHITECTS

→ →

179 top ■ The Atelier Brancusi, designed by Renzo Piano in the 1990s, completes the square, reviving the mood of the late artist's workshop.

Place George Pompidou thus plays a role of mediation between the scale of the building, the scale of the Marais district and that of the city: immersed in it, visitors are subjected to Beaubourg's structural hypertechnology, which in reality conceals an ancient artisanal spirit that derives from its having been made piece by piece, produced industrially, but in the perspective of this one scheme. Escalators applied to the exterior carry visitors upwards, gradually removing them from the square, packed with tourists and mimes, musicians and artists, until the Paris skyline comes into view, and they can gaze either across the city, toward the spires of Nôtre-Dame, or down over the immediate vicinity. Plateau Beaubourg, adjacent to the building and with its other three sides demarcated by Rue Rambuteau, Rue Saint-Martin and Rue Saint-Merri, is a large rectangular reception space that serves as a foyer but also as the continuation of the Centre Pompidou. It is above all an integral part of the urban plan structured to accommodate entertainment and culture, due to its connections with IRCAM, the institute for research and coordination of acoustics and music, and with the Atelier Brancusi.

178-179 ■ The underground car park's ventilation ducts rise out of the square's slightly sloping plane like periscopes.

179 bottom ■ Traditional Parisian architecture interacts with Beaubourg's techno-mechanical composite: a popular tourist attraction.

Across Rue Saint-Merri is another square whose underground area conceals the physical and conceptual "rib" of the Centre Pompidou: IRCAM, which was also designed by the Studio Piano & Rogers. The Atelier of Romanian sculptor Constantin Brancusi faces directly onto the Plateau, and was positioned at one corner of the square, by Renzo Piano so as to underscore the strong bond that already existed among the various types of artistic expression celebrated by the Centre. In the 1990s, the architect added a transparent canopy to protect the new entrance from the plateau into the building's ground floor: the ample façade, also transparent, soars up from here, traced by enormous translucent tubes that hold the escalators, while massive air-conditioning conduits for the three underground floors emerge like periscopes from the plaza's geometrically designed paving stones.

180-181 ■ The Centre Pompidou's technological feature is completely evident, especially at night, thanks to the lighting that projects the interiors outwards.

181 bottom ■ The square's lengthwise section shows the underground car park and how close the complex is to IRCAM, conceived to enjoy a close bond with the museum.

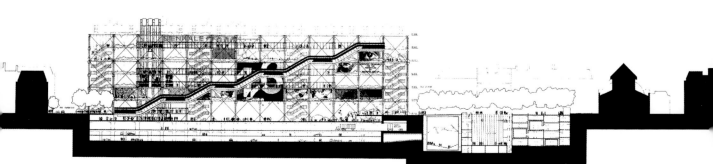

TSUKUBA CENTER
SQUARE

[TSUKUBA ■ JAPAN]

Tsukuba Center Square was inspired by Rome's Capitol Square and is the result of Arata Isozaki's unique architectural manner. The plaza lies the heart of Tsukuba, a new city center theoretically designed in 1963 to relieve overpopulation pressure in nearby Tokyo. Tsukuba, about 40 miles (60 kilometers) away, was conceived by the Japan Housing Corporation and intended as a place to move all the university research and administrative structures found in Tokyo and group them together in a single scientific hub. The Japan Housing Corporation did not just define a specialist agglomeration, as required by the university, but also imagined residential development, and consequently included collective, commercial, and cultural infrastructures, so that the town was able to be entirely independent of neighboring urban centers: an outright "City of Science."

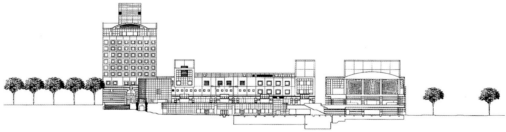

182-183 and 183 center ■ The drawing above shows a ruined square, symbolizing
the architect's bond with Western culture and awareness of the past tragic events.
Below, the section is structured along the horizontal axis of the complex.

183 bottom ■ The image shows the sequence of constructions set around the square.

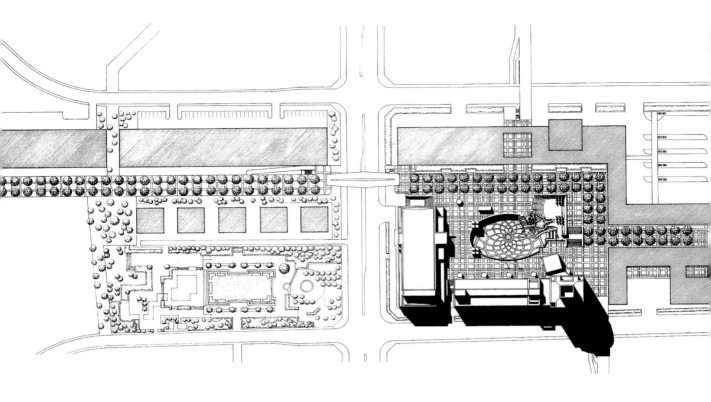

To give life to this scheme, an invitation-only competition was held to seek an architect who would realize the central civic complex, a recreational area, and a community rendezvous point with distinctive, eye-catching appeal. The winner was Arata Isozaki, Japan's second most famous architect abroad after Kenzo Tange, and an artist capable of alluding to the history of Western architecture to express modern-day Japanese culture. Not surprisingly, Isozaki brought in the square, an iconic element of socialization and life in Western towns, and used it as the focal point of the complex, installing a hotel, a concert hall, a recreational area, and a shopping mall.

The square is built on a rectangular slab that is the first overground level of the civic complex and, is zigzagged by Tsukuba's major transportation axes. The raised slab is higher than the vehicular traffic arteries and can be reached by pedestrian bridges suspended over the roads.

The square's paving fabric comprises three offset geometrical grids in different colors, dotted with greenery, separating in the center to plunge into the hollow ellipse, in homage to Michelangelo's Piazza del Campidoglio in Rome.

The "high" square leads down to the "low" one via a ramp with irregular steps that evoke the natural slope of the terrain, and accommodated by rocks that reach a fountain and encircle a small open-air cavea. The shopping mall's windows face out onto the stellar Michelangelo tribute, while on the upper level, on two sides of the high square, there are

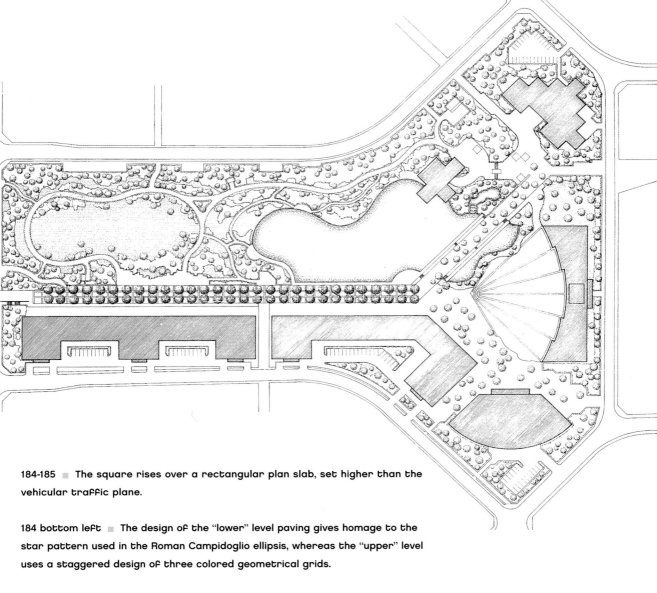

184-185 ■ The square rises over a rectangular plan slab, set higher than the vehicular traffic plane.

184 bottom left ■ The design of the "lower" level paving gives homage to the star pattern used in the Roman Campidoglio ellipsis, whereas the "upper" level uses a staggered design of three colored geometrical grids.

184 bottom right ■ A fountain soars over the center of elliptical plaza.

LOCATION	YEAR OF CONSTRUCTION	AREA	APPLICATION	PROJECT
TSUKUBA (JAPAN)	1979-1983	39,000 SQ FEET	CIVIC AND COMMERCIAL SQUARE	ARATA ISOZAKI

two horizontal parallelepiped blocks and a hotel tower, where a small cube encloses a dining room.

Opposite the cube is a classical allusion, a sculpture by Hidetoshi Nagasawa named *Daphne turned to laurel to escape Apollo*. Even the buildings on the square are characterized by elements borrowed from the Western architectural tradition, which Isozaki overlaps in a fragmentary way, an ironic attitude he himself has defined as "schizophrenic eclecticism." Thus, local granite ashlar bases allude to the tradition of Renaissance buildings, but support smooth façades in silver tiles, some polished, some matte, and aluminum panels. The jutting concert hall frontage pierced by a triangular opening alludes to the pronaos of a temple, but the columns beneath have drums of different sizes and that seem to have been purloined from the saltpan custodian's house at Chaux di Claude-Nicolas Ledoux. The architect feels that each motif is independent and retains its distinctive nature; in Isozaki's own words, the Center "represents an attempt to deconstruct Western elements using Japanese elements."

The illustration of the square and its buildings derelict, almost devastated by an earthquake, is also an quotation from Western architectural history: on one hand evoking John Soane's Neoclassical Bank of England depicted in the same way, but on the other a commemoration of "grief for what has gone... Hiroshima, the Holocaust", in the awareness that the future will one day become a ruin.

PLACE DU
NOMBRE D'OR

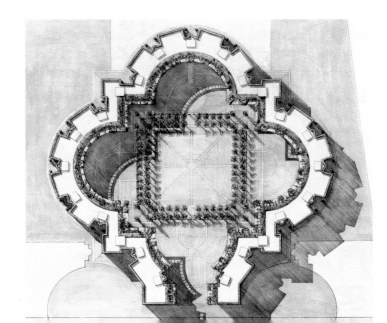

186-187 ■ The heart of the "Antigone" residential and services complex, commissioned by the Montpellier City Council in the Eighties, is the monumental Place du Nombre d'Or, by Ricardo Bofill's Taller de Arquitectura.

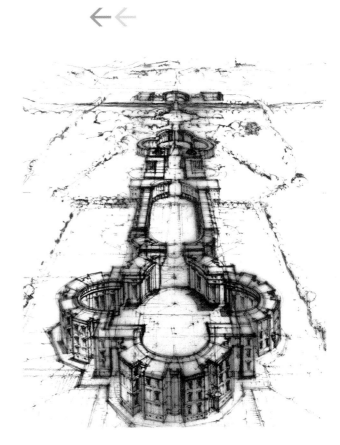

Place du Nombre d'Or is the fulcrum of Antigone, an entire sector of contemporary city commissioned by Montpellier in the late 1970s and executed by the Catalan architect Ricardo Bofill and his multidisciplinary team, Taller de Arquitectura, In fact, the site was the result of a decision to regulate development of the entire city eastwards, toward the banks of the River Lez and recovering its relations with the water course. The intention was to avoid the same sort of error committed in the 1960s, when the municipal council had purchased a vast area at the back of Montpellier city center and had started to build a trade center called Polygone, which was heavily criticized for its anonymity. Consequently the need arose to plan a new intervention, and it was entrusted to Bofill and his team, already well-known in France for their *villes nouvelles* schemes in Cergy-Pontoise and Saint Quentin en Yvelin, which were realized in 1971 and 1973, respectively. The residential and services center, called Antigone, was conceived and given this name to reflect the architect's intentions: this Greek heroine serves as an allusion to the designer's conceptual attitude, the projection of undifferentiated chaos generated by settlements lacking proper planning, offset with historical urban design criteria.

186 bottom and 187 ■ The Place du Nombre d'Or layout and a perspective of the entire intervention, showing the the square's multilobed outline, installed at the end of a complex sequence.

188 top ■ The square's curved frontage reaches a height of seven stories.

The composition of Antigone reflects the principles of Baroque city planning, treating each building as a piece of a mosaic, repeated to compose an urban scenario, and making use of classical architectural style features including columns, tympana and friezes, to express thought processes. The kingpin of the complex, arranged in a sequence of geometrical plazas, founded on proportions derived from application of the Golden Ratio, is Place du Nombre d'Or, behind which Polygone pales into insignificance. The plan conceived by the Taller de Arquitectura rolls from here down to the banks of the River Lez, developed on a straight axis along which the sequence of squares flow into one another, beginning at Place du Nombre d'Or. Each is based on the elaboration of elementary geometrical figures: the square, the rectangle, the polygon and the circle.

Place du Nombre d'Or is the zenith, founded on a square matrix and embraced by an uninterrupted curtain wall that curves to either side, to form four semicircular exedras, and is broken only by the opening into the next plaza; this has a rectangular plan with rounded corners, and is called *Les Echelles de la Ville*. It connects to the polygonal plaza, transformed by a trilobate layout, which then leads into the massive semicircle overlooking the banks of the River Lez.

Observed from inside Place du Nombre d'Or, the buildings around its perimeter offer a continuum of seven levels, whereas from the exterior, the individual buildings are evident. Four passageways are installed at the corners of the base square, at ground level, to allow residents free access to the plaza, which is paved and provided with a baluster that shadows its square layout, while the main axis is highlighted by paired columns supporting a tympanum. A row of leafy trees is also present, to underscore the geometry of the square, a mediator between the monumental scale of the buildings and the human dimension. Giant ochre cement pilaster strips cadence the façades, closing in a heavily jutting cornice that is anchored to the structure by surprisingly slender supports. Massive tripartite string courses and a denticulate frieze englobe small windows and overlap the pilaster strips, among which ample gable windows are set at intervals. The space occupied by the square thus appears as a sequence of curves and right angles, with forceful prefabricated cement columns set at the joining point – a remarkable depiction of the fusion of magnificent classical architecture with sophisticated leading-edge technology.

188 bottom ■ The square complex develops vertically, using the elements of Classical architecture: columns, tympanums, cornices, which underscore the use of the Golden Section in layout studies.

189 ■ The gigantic cornice soars over 16 feet above the roof, creating a distinctive contrast of light and shade.

LOCATION	YEAR OF CONSTRUCTION	AREA	APPLICATION	PROJECT
MONTPELLIER (FRANCE)	1979-1985	APPROXIMATELY 82,000 SQ FEET	SYSTEM OF SQUARES	RICARDO BOFILL TALLER DE ARQUITECTURA

189 SAN MARCO

PLAÇA DELS
PAÏSOS CATALANS

[BARCELONA ■ SPAIN]

190-191 ■ The square's jagged skyline, offset by the rippling marquise, traces the way to Sants Station and the platform roof offering shelter there.

Plaça dels Països Catalans, better known as the Sants Station square, was the first project to have been completed as part of a public area refurbishment scheme that Barcelona city council initiated in 1980 with the establishment of the "Servei de Projectes

190 bottom ■ The square's perspective underscores the roles of the marquise and the platform roof as urban furnishing elements.

191 ■ Dancing fountains flank the path to the station and suggest an gratifying function for the square.

Urbans," under the direction of Oriol Bohigas. Planning "by fragments" that involved not only the city center, but also the suburbs, it focused specifically on the recovery of degraded areas and urban voids, as well as the creation of brand new plazas.

The redesign of Plaça dels Països Catalans was entrusted to the firm of Viaplana/Piñón arqts., and was one of the cases where refurbishment targeted the enhancement of parts of the city lacking in appeal. What is now a brilliantly executed result was then a challenge that the architects were hard put to meet, since the site was hampered on the surface by lanes of fast traffic and underground by the train lines entering Sants Station. In fact, the area under the square is crossed by tracks and could not support heavy building structures or be weakened by tree plantings or the installation of gardens. Moreover, the site suffered from a dull and lopsided layout, with buildings of varying heights, from two to six floors, and different uses, so that it failed to present a coherent and unified urban scenario.

Today the plaza is an abstract space, filled with metal objects and furnishings. The ordered harmony offsets the existing cityscape and allows glimpses of Parc de L'Espanya Industrial, with its monumental tower-lighting elements. In this way the square interacts with another important intervention of the early Eighties undertaken by Luis Peña Ganchegui and Francesc Rius i Camps, and thus forges the actions commissioned by public administration into a single link.

192 top ■ The shadows cast by the sun's rays on the paving highlight the soft curves of the marquise, benches serving as seating and tables offer tourists and travelers a place to rest.

192-193 ■ The jets of water are sprayed from vertical elements, set elegantly into the system of aerial frames that define the square's layout.

192 bottom ■ The prospect shows clearly the vertical frame of the marquise, flanked by the rippling horizontal line of the platform roof.

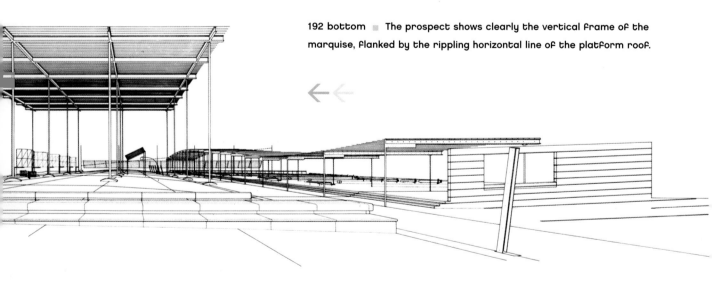

Plaça dels Països Catalans is brought to life by a platform roof, a pathway with an undulated canopy, benches, water jets, and lighting elements, all laid out in an understated system where each item retains its individuality yet is integral with the whole. Pink granite paving carpets the plaza's enormous flat surface and is crossed by agile walkways that combine with the metal furnishings to guide travelers towards the lower level, the location of the low, square station building. In point of fact, the architects accepted the area's irregular geometry but compensated for it by accentuating the ideal continuation of the largest of the roads converging on the plaza

LOCATION	YEAR OF CONSTRUCTION	AREA	APPLICATION	PROJECT
BARCELONA (SPAIN)	1981-1983	APPROXIMATELY 112,000 SQ FEET	TRAFFIC SQUARE	ALBERT VIAPLANA I VEÀ VIAPLANA/PIÑÓN ARQTS.

with a preferential channel towards the station itself. The platform roof is a further statement in this sense: it leads directly to the station entrance and, at the same time, its curving roof creates a unique shadow play on the paving, cadencing the path taken by the tourists. Granite benches, designed as seating or tables, are installed under the platform roof, and offer arriving or departing travelers a moment of respite. The roof splits the square into two sections: one is completely free, set with an uninterrupted series of black basalt benches that appear as a sinuous wave reaching towards the building if observed from above; the other is occupied by a canopy set on 16 slim metal pilasters and opening out towards Parc de L'Espanya Industrial. The canopy is lit from below by a special panel, tilted to a 30° angle and the lighting is actually a decisive factor in guiding travelers in the dark: special tall lampposts map out the square's main pathways and a series of short pillars escort the height changes.

The plaza also has a fountain, a sequence of steel spheres, and a series of sculpted pieces that contribute to the creation of an abstract picture of pure, original beauty. This installation won the 1983 *Foment de les Arts Decoratives*, an architecture award, as well as the *Ciutat de Barcelona* prize.

PARLIAMENT
SQUARE

[CANBERRA ■ AUSTRALIA]

194-195 ■ The aerial view highlights the virtual axis that connects the Old Parliament, seen in the foreground, to the New, in the background, preceded by the square.

195 ■ Australia's state flag fluttering above Parliament's entrance portico, decorated with the national icons: a kangaroo and an emu.

The square in front of Parliament House in Canberra, as well as the complex where it is located, is crucially significant to Australian culture and history. In fact, the site, which was designed as a symbol of national unity and democratic freedom, was inaugurated in 1988 during the bicentennial celebrations of the first stable British settlement in Australia, and the replacement of Old Parliament House, dating back to 1927. The square represents what the construction of the entire city had stood for in the early 1900s, when Canberra was conceived as an *ex novo* capital of the new federal state. Since Sydney and Melbourne were contenders for the role, the new Constitution solved the dispute by deciding that the country's political and administrative center ought to be erected in New South Wales, and once the site was decided, an international competition was held to design the urban center. This is how Canberra, which means "meeting place" in Aborigine dialect, was born.

Over 130 projects were presented, and the winner was a 35-year-old American architect, Walter Burley Griffin, who cleverly understood the landscape potential of the location and exploited it for his ideas. In specific, he planned a garden city arranged along the

194 bottom ■ The New Parliament, set into Capital Hill, opens into the trapezoidal plaza, which leads into the entire complex.

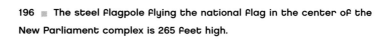

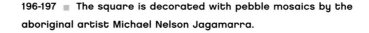

196 ■ The steel flagpole flying the national flag in the center of the New Parliament complex is 265 feet high.

196-197 ■ The square is decorated with pebble mosaics by the aboriginal artist Michael Nelson Jagamarra.

shores of an artificial lake created by damming the waters of the River Molonglo. The urban area was organized around the physical and conceptual fulcrum, Capital Hill, which is the vertex of "Parliament Triangle," with Commonwealth Avenue and Kings Avenue making up the sides of an ideal equilateral triangle whose base is the curving Parkes Way. These two avenues, along with Adelaide, Melbourne and Canberra Avenues – flow directly into Capital Circle, the road loop that surrounds New Parliament House. This is the home of the Australian Government and was designed by Mitchell/Giurgola & Thorp Architects. The building, merging into the original profile of Capital Hill, interacts with the main axes of Burley Griffin's plans: it is aligned with the vertical axis that connects Old Parliament House to the Australian Memorial War; set beyond Burley Griffin's lake, which in turn is the city's horizontal axis, on which "Parliament Triangle" lies.

The spectacular New Parliament House comprises three blocks within a square plan, and surrounds a trapezoidal plaza separated from vehicular traffic and connected by a system of garden terraces to the old Parliament and the banks of the lake. Also designed by Mitchell/Giurgola & Thorp, this square greets employees, parliamentarians, tourists,

LOCATION	YEAR OF CONSTRUCTION	AREA	APPLICATION	PROJECT
CANBERRA (AUSTRALIA)	1988	APPROXIMATELY 124,000 SQ FEET	CIVIC SQUARE	MITCHELL/GIURGOLA & THORP ARCHITECTS

and visitors with an open space that leads into the foyer of the complex, and hence into the Great Hall, a huge hospitality area, the council chambers and the mighty side buildings, which are bordered by curving walls and separated by lawns and flowerbeds. In front of the foyer, an access portico acts as a backdrop to the plaza. A symmetrical mass with twenty white marble-faced supporting pillars rounding outward at the center, it serves (like the building) not only as a workplace, but also as a symbol of the nation and a ceremonial venue. It is decorated with a red gravel mosaic crafted by local artist Michael Nelson Jagamarra, anticipating installations and other works of art set in the building proper which were created to commemorate and reflect the history of the Australian people from pre-colonial times to the present day.

The plaza, which slopes slightly downward, mimics the layout of the city around it: Nelson Jagamarra's mosaic is installed where the avenues meet, inscribed in a square and surrounded by a pool of water that reflects the whiteness of the portico, contrasting with the brick-colored paving. Its civic significance is made even more apparent by the giant steel flagpole that soars from the center of the rear building

CALIFORNIA
PLAZA

[LOS ANGELES ■ USA]

198 ■ The main space
in California Plaza is
encircled by the three
soaring glass office
towers, with the
underground levels
of the building complex
looking out onto it.

199 top ■ A sequence of
benches is set amongst
the trees and bushes,
with fountains around the
bases of the towers and
the path to the MoCa.

199 bottom ■ The MoCa,
Los Angeles' Museum
of Contemporary Art,
overlooks the sculpture
courtyard, towards
California Plaza.

California Plaza is the result of a colossal financial scheme for urban redesign and a testimony to the vision of Arthur Erickson & Associates, the Canadian architectural firm who skillful interpreted the demands of its client, Los Angeles CRA (Community Redevelopment Agency). The project, which took ten years to complete, and an investment of two billion dollars, redefined the layout of the city's vast Bunker Hill area, covering about 11.2 acres (45,300 square meters) in the heart of the metropolis, between the northeast corner of Grand Avenue and Fourth Street. Erickson took on the job after successfully entering a 1980 competition held by the CRA; and his winning design was underpinned by a synergic vision of several judged components, including the optimized distribution of private and tourist accommodation, service and trade, and an allocation of at least 1.5% of the budget for public schemes like museums, galleries, and other venues for cultural and artistic endeavors.

The competition coincided with a significant occurrence: the Community Redevelopment Agency's decision to create a museum dedicated solely to contemporary art. Having been alerted (like the other teams of backers and designers involved) to this requirement, Erickson set about his plan of laying out the entire complex so as to exploit the ground floor by installing a series of courts and buildings that reached both above and beneath street level. Later two office block towers were added: One and Two California Plazas. The former was inaugurated in 1986 together with MoCa, Japanese architect Arata Isozaki's Museum of Contemporary Art.

200-201 ■ The small, terraced amphitheater in California Plaza slopes down by one floor, opening into an irregular space with flowerbeds and fountains.

Erickson placed the two skyscrapers at the base of the plot, arranging a series of open spaces that form California Plaza and were conceived to be the connective tissue for offices, a luxury hotel, residences, MoCa, and the Dance Gallery, a performing arts theater designed by the Bella Lewitsky group and built at a later date.

Soon afterward, the plaza became the fulcrum of an intervention which made substantial modifications to a portion of downtown Los Angeles (and contributed significantly to the city's system of open spaces) by forging a conceptual connection with the Music Center, which stands at the symbolic heart of the metropolis, Pershing Square. Angel's Flight, the early-1900s cable car that once ferried tourists and residents up and own the hillside, was also restored and brought back into the fabric of the community.

Over the 1990s, California Plaza grew into a public space that unfolded at different heights, amidst soaring glass and steel towers and the famous Museum of Contemporary Art, distinguished by its sandstone cubes, pyramids and barrel vaults set onto a red sandstone base. Observed from Grand Avenue, the museum comprises two blocks separated by the sculpture courtyard, which is really the core of the museum apparatus, and includes offices and a bookstore opening directly onto the square. Meanwhile, access to the exhibition rooms is through a courtyard set lower down, at the height defined by the overlying California Plaza. The museum is built partly above and partly below the plaza's own car park, and conceals the Dance Gallery, whose entrance is marked by a tall iron and glass structure with a jagged, spiraling profile, lit up at night.

California Plaza contains a garden with pools and fountains, ornamental plants and tree-lined courts, embedded between MoCa and the first office tower. The square features a semicircular terraced ramp that rolls down to the shopping arcade under the offices and provides a pleasing milieu of lush vegetation, ideal for resting during a busy day. Equally unique, but more sumptuous, is the court fitted between the two office towers, created with the assistance of artist David Hockey: a pool of water at the end of a cavea that has been dug at the foot of the tower blocks and surrounded by pavilions that are specially lit up at night.

LOCATION	YEAR OF CONSTRUCTION	AREA	APPLICATION	PROJECT
LOS ANGELES (USA)	1980-1990	APPROXIMATELY 1,302,000 SQ FEET	CIVIC SQUARE	ARTHUR ERICKSON & ASSOCIATES

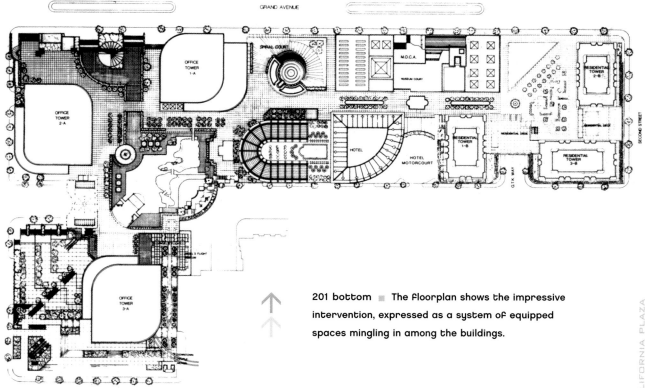

201 bottom ■ The floorplan shows the impressive intervention, expressed as a system of equipped spaces mingling in among the buildings.

SCHOUWBURGPLEIN

[ROTTERDAM ■ THE NETHERLANDS]

Schouwburgplein, which is close to the central train station in the heart of Rotterdam, is a vast square and one of the most important in the city; in addition it bears the distinctive identity given it by the presence of Europe's biggest port infrastructure. The square was neglected for many years, despite its amenable position, and it was not until the early 1990s that it was targeted by the city council, who initially decided on a recovery intervention, beginning with the façades that delineate its large, rectangular shape.

The urban planning and landscaping firm West 8 was consulted for this initial scheme, and made a counter-proposal to valorize the void amidst the buildings, redesign the paving area, and renew the square's functions.

In fact, West 8, predicates its work on the awareness that the contemporary landscape is mainly artificial, manipulated by human beings and comprising components of varying types, which may be re-utilized to better respond to collective needs. That is why, in the Schouwburgplein intervention, the use of technology and the fast pace of modern life was accepted with composure, and merged positively and playfully, with the intention of persuading citizens to occupy and interact with the urban space.

The square is conceived as a large foyer for the cultural institutions located there: the Schouwburg Opera House, after which the square is named, the De Doelen Concert Hall, and Bioscoop, a multiplex cinema designed by Koen van Velsen in 1990.

202 ■ Tourists and residents crowd the interactive space of Schouwburgplein, Rotterdam's new central square, built in the 1990s.

203 ■ Huge mechanical elements, painted red and lined up along the edge of the square form a lighting system; they are flanked by benches and ventilation towers.

Since there are also numerous offices, stores and dwellings, the square is crowded day and night, and the architects aimed to answer the flexible requirements of various times of the day and of different users: children, teenagers, adults, and the elderly.

As a result, the square can be a place to rest, a place to meet, a place to play, or a venue for concerts, public performances, and sports events.

It was to this end that West 8 configured the layout as a sort of citizens' stage, where "players" cross the square or use its facilities, perceived either as stars of ordinary city life, or spectators lingering on benches and in recreation areas.

Schouwburgplein is a rectangle, with the De Doelen Concert Hall on the north side, the opera house opposite, on the south side, and stores and offices to the east and west. The more recent cinema complex, an eye-catching feature in the evenings with its bright façade, was built at the corner of the rectangle that forms the square.

The cinema's translucent coating accentuates the suggestive, scenographic effect of the specific lighting system used for the entire project. Four enormous articulated red lighting masts are aligned on one side of the square, bearing such a strong resemblance to the port of Rotterdam's hydraulic cranes that Schouwburgplein could be mistaken for an oil rig or an artificial island. The lighting can be activated by the public, using special controls, so they can, for instance, spotlight their heroes during a sports event.

Three tall, reticular towers containing ventilation plants for the large underground car park rise out of the ground to provide a further source of light at night. Observed as a whole, these towers create a digital clock that shows hours, minutes and seconds.

204 ■ The square's paving is characteristic for its use of different materials to suggest the intended use of each area: wood for rest areas, steel panels and resin sheets for the skating area.

204-205 ■ The urban showcase of Schouwburgplein by night, lit against the Bioscoop multiscreen cinema backdrop.

205 bottom ■ The aerial view shows the Schouwburgplein complex during a show, gleaming with lights and color.

LOCATION	YEAR OF CONSTRUCTION	AREA	APPLICATION	PROJECT
ROTTERDAM (NETHERLANDS)	1991-1997	APPROXIMATELY 132,000 SQ FEET	CIVIC SQUARE - URBAN STAGE	WEST 8

Triangular glass prisms connect the ground level with the underlying floors. The square rises about 14 inches (35 centimeters) at the point of the underground car park and creates the impression of a floating surface suspended over the terrain. In fact, at its center, the paving is finished with perforated metal panels that are lit from below with white, green, and black fluorescent tubes. Next to this, also in the center of the square, are wooden slats laid in a herringbone design to map out a play area; along the west side, resin slabs with metal leaves have been used; and on the east side, the sunniest, where geraniums flower in summer, there are rubber panels and a continuous series of shaped wooden seats.

The paving system features an unusual combination of different materials: wood, metal, rubber and resin create a mosaic whose layout adapts to varying intensities of sunlight, true to the West 8 design incentive of interpreting changing weather conditions. Rows of trees set along the main traffic street skirt the square and act as a filter, with surrounding buildings rising behind them.

With Schouwburgplein, the West 8 studio successfully put together the image of a lively industrial city, looking to the new millennium and taking its cues from Rotterdam's industrial setting to accentuate a technological and sensational look.

POTSDAMER

PLATZ

[BERLIN ▪ GERMANY]

206 bottom ▪ The view shows the sequence of buildings designed by Renzo Piano, with the eye-catching B1 office block, with glass cladding, the surviving Weinhaushut, the IMAX cupola up to the Debis tower.

206-207 ■ The Potsdamer Platz area shows a number of architectural interventions: the complex, conceived by Renzo Piano, extends up to the Landwehrkanal; in the foreground, the Philharmonic, Hans Scharoun's national library, and Helmut Jahn's Sony Center.

207 ■ The sketch by Renzo Piano describes the founding principles of the project: the Tiergarten and the Kulturforum are urban elements which, together with the Landeskanal, are linked to Potsdamer Platz. The future Marlene Dietrich Platz, heart of the intervention, is seen to emerge.

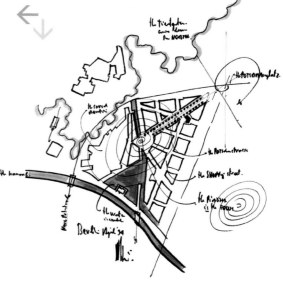

It was the 1990s, and behind the Kulturforum complex of Mies van der Rohe's new national gallery, the Philharmonic and Hans Scharoun's national library, the urban void of Potsdamer Platz lingered in Berlin, the destruction of the Berlin Wall revealing its entire moral and material bleakness. Decades earlier, in the years before the Second World War, the square has been a symbol of social life, the ferment of culture, and mercantile trade, but during the war years it was razed by devastating bombing, and immediately after the war it was demolished according to plans that were s intended to wipe out all traces of the recent, dramatic past. The building of the wall at the edge of this square in the east of Berlin confirmed its abandon and, in 1972, the erection of the national library to the west provided further proof of the separation, considering the element a "definitive" social and architectural splitting of the two halves of the capital.

The future of Potsdamer Platz brightened only when, following the unification of Germany and the demolition of the Berlin Wall, a competition was held to select a designer for reconstruction of the vast Potsdamer Platz area.

The winner was the Renzo Piano Building Workshop, and the project was sponsored by Daimler-Chrysler. The entire area, except for the Weinhaushut and the old Potsdamer Strasse route with its double row of lindens, which had been under protection since the 1950s, had to be designed *ex novo*. Piano's main objective was to "heal the wound" that the Wall had left in the urban fabric, creating

208-209 ■ The spectacular
glass and steel cupola,
designed by architect
Helmut Jahn for the
huge Sony Center,
at the entrance to
Potsdamer Platz.

208 bottom ■ Helmut
Jahn's Sony Center
encloses a kind of covered
foyer that serves as
a distribution point for
the complex's various
services and, thanks to
a central pool of water,
it is also a spot for
meeting and relaxing.

the "missing tessera" the city had lost, with all its functions and its daily vitality. Mindful of Berlin's history and urban layout, Piano used nature, in other words the trees, to connect the great green lung of the Tiergarten to the Kulturforum by treating it as an offshoot that extended to Potsdamer

Platz; and by seeing the latter as a further extension to the Landwehrkanal, via an artificial lake.

Water penetrated the area, cutting through the heart of the operation, the new square around which the 18-building complex was installed, with eight buildings entrusted to the Renzo Piano Building Workshop, including the new head offices of the sponsor, Daimler-Chrysler. To the east and to the north, blocks were arranged in compliance with city plans. For his part, Piano introduced the

LOCATION	YEAR OF CONSTRUCTION	AREA	APPLICATION	PROJECT
BERLIN (GERMANY)	1992-2000	APPROXIMATELY 64,600 SQ FEET	CIVIC SQUARE	RENZO PIANO BUILDING WORKSHOP

principle of "coherence without uniformity", nuancing building façades through the use of a variety of terracotta features that created the illusion of a single but diversified environment.

Today the success of the architect's intentions is evident, and the new square, renamed Marlene Dietrich Platz, has become the hinge between the Kulturforum and Alte Potsdamer Strasse, serving as a sort of "barycenter of aggregation," that vibrates with activity both day and night, since the area is home to a hotel, a casino, a theatre, a movie theater, restaurants, offices, and dwellings. The irregular outline is lapped by the water of the artificial lake, whose surface reflects and lifts the volumes of the surrounding buildings, which include the metal-clad theater and casino, next to the powerful mass of the national library. An office complex, topped with the tall Debis tower (a Daimler-Benz group company) stands next to the water, with the tower's matte clay and gleaming glass soaring skywards. Restaurants and an art gallery are located at ground level and in the restored Weinhaushut. The plaza is also

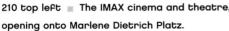

210 top left ■ The IMAX cinema and theatre, opening onto Marlene Dietrich Platz.

210 top right ■ The Philharmonic's curving mass looks out from the Kulturforum.

the location of the angular, panoramic IMAX cinema, immediately recognizable by to its semi-circular, ceramic-tile finish front, as if some spherical meteorite had tumbled into the foyer, lighting up at night to bounce back moonbeams. Opposite there is a residential building with a court encircling a garden. Restaurants and stores are located in the lower section, and continue into the rear arcade, offering late closing times for evening shoppers. The first building erected here was about 200 feet in height – a rangy office block with a double ter-racotta-glass cladding, set at the northeast tip of Alte Potsdamer Strasse.

The entire Potsdamer Platz complex is a testimony to the intelligent direction taken by the Renzo Piano Building Workshop, skillfully blending its own actions with those of architects like Hans Kollhoff, José Rafael Moneo, Richard Rogers, Arata Isozaki and Lauber + Wöhr, deciding on the use of similar materials throughout, to ensure unison but producing variety. Most significant, the site's wealth of functions give it the vitality that typified it before World War II, and have thus restored it to its former place in the ranks of Berlin's best-loved public spaces.

210 bottom ■ The subway entrance flanks the glass prow of the B1 building, the first to be designed by Renzo Piano's Building Workshop.

211 ■ Interwoven brick unifies the entire Potsdamer Platz project, including the IMAX cinema with its curved front and huge cupola.

essential bibliography

Il Campidoglio di Michelangelo, Silvana Editoriale d'Arte, Milan 1965.

Enrico Guidoni, *Il Campo di Siena*, Multigrafica ed., Rome 1971.

Paolo Favole, *Piazze d'Italia: architettura e urbanistica della piazza in Italia*, Bramante, Milan 1972.

José Augusto França, *Una città dell'illuminismo. La Lisbona del marchese Pombal*, Officina edizioni, Rome 1972.

Piazza del Duomo a Milano: storia, problemi, progetti, Mazzotta, Milan 1982.

Giuseppe Samonà, *Piazza San Marco: l'architettura, la storia, le funzioni*, Marsilio (3ª edizione), Venice 1982.

Renzo Piano, Richard Rogers, *Du Plateau Beaubourg au Centre G. Pompidou*, Editions du Centre Pompidou, Paris 1987.

Valnea Santa Maria Scrinari, Bianca Maria Favetta, Gaia Furlan, *Piazza Unità d'Italia a Trieste*, B & M Fachin, Trieste 1990.

New architecture. Squares, vol. 6, Atrium, Barcelona 1992.

Edgard Goedleven, *La Grand-Place de Bruxelles*, Racine, Bruxelles 1993.

Paolo Favole, *Piazze nell'architettura contemporanea*, Federico Motta, Milan 1995.

De la place royale à la place des Vosges, Action Artistique de la ville de Paris. Académie d'architecture, Paris 1996.

Rochelle Ziskin, *The Place Vendôme*, Cambridge University Press, Cambridge and New York 1999.

Giovanni Di Lorenzo, Mark Münzing, *Potsdamer Platz Project 1989 to 2000*, Karl Schlögel, Daimler Chrysler Immobilien (DCI), Berlin 2001.

Ferruccio Lombardi, *Le piazze storiche di Roma esistenti e scomparse*, Newton & Compton, Rome 2001.

Plätze und städtische Freiräume von 1993 bis heute, Munich: Callwey Verlag; Basel: Birkhäuser 2002.

Jan Gehl, Lars Gemzøe, *New city spaces*, The Danish architectural press (3rd edition), Copenhagen 2003.

Pietro Carlo Pellegrini, *Piazze e spazi pubblici: architetture 1990-2005*, Federico Motta, Milan 2005.

index

c = caption   boldface = specific chapter

index

index

photographic credits

photographic credits

Kord.com/Agefotostock/ Contrasto: pages 152-153, 154
Robert Landau/Corbis: page 157 (5th photo)
Dirk Laubner: pages 30-31, 94-95, 136-137
Dieter Leistner/Artur: page 7
Marcello Libra/Archivio White Star: pages 26 top, 29 top and bottom, 30, 32-33, 136, 139, 141, 142, 142-143
London Aerial Photo Library/ Corbis: page 15 (3rd photo)
Melvyn Longhurst/Alamy: pages 145 top and bottom
Fritz Mader/Sime/Sie: page 208
R. Matina/Agefotostock/Marka: page 127 bottom
Martin Mehlig/Sime/Sie: pages 138-139
James Montgomery/Sime/Sie: page 159
Andrew Moore: page 121
James H. Morris: page 157 (4th photo)
Jeroen Musch: pages 202, 203, 204-205, 205
Museum of Finnish Architecture, Helsinki: pages 166 top and bottom, 170
David Noton/Agefotostock/ Contrasto: page 125
Steven Nowakowski/OzImages: page 196
Kevin O' Hara/Agefotostock/ Marka: pages 86, 87
Werner Otto/Agefotostock/ Contrasto: page 115 top
Werner Otto/Agefotostock/ Marka: page 96
Vladimir Pcholkin/Agefotostock/ Contrasto: pages 88-89
David Peevers/Lonely Planet Images: page 211
Bruno Perousse/Agefotostock/ Marka: pages 170-171
Bruno Perousse/Hoa-Qui/ Hachette Photos/Contrasto: page 90

Peter Phipp/Travelshots.com: page 110
Photolibrary Group: pages 10-11, 148-149, 172-173
Photos12.com: page 178
Photoservice Electa: pages 44, 129
Photoservice Electa/AKG Images: pages 15 (6th photo), 106-107, 112 top and bottom, 112-113, 116
Marco Pierfranceschi/Vision: page 71 top
Fabio Pili/Alamy: page 165 right
Sergio Pitamitz/DanitaDelimont: pages 92-93
Pubbli Aer Foto: pages 44-45
Massimo Ripani/Sime/Sie: pages 76-77
Gustavo Rizzi/Fotoscopio: page 101
Martin Rugner/Agefotostock/ Marka: page 137
Studio Erick Saillet: pages 84, 84-85
E. Sampers/Explorer/ Hoa-Qui/Hachette Photos/ Contrasto: pages 122-123
David Sanger Photography/ Alamy: pages 18-19
Santos/zefa/Corbis page 210 top left
Sebastiano Scattolin/Sime/Sie: pages 42-43
Alain Schein Photography/Corbis: page 155
Reinhard Schmid/Sime/Sie: pages 96-97
Doug Scott/Agefotostock/Marka: page 164
Neil Setchfield/Lonely Planet Imges: page 35
Giovanni Simeone/Sime/Sie: pages 5, 20-21, 24-25, 47, 56-57, 62, 70-71
Henri Stierlin: pages 58-59
Stockfolio/Alamy: page 104
Rudy Sulgan/Corbis: pages 154-155
Michele Tabozzi: pages 179 bottom, 180-181

Penny Tweedie/Corbis: pages 196-197
Giulio Veggi/Archivio White Star: pages 23 top, 26 bottom, 28-29, 46, 71 bottom, 109, 120, 157 (7th photo)
Steve Vidler/Agefotostock/ Marka: page 157 (1st photo)
Visual Arts Library (London)/Alamy: page 80
Julia Waterlow; Eye Ubiquitous/ Corbis: pages 164-165
Ken Welsh/Agefotostock/ Contrasto: pages 100-101
World Pictures/Photoshot: page 148
Richard JW Wright: pages 199 top and bottom
Michael Yamashita: page 152
Bruce Yuan-Yue Bi/Lonely Planet Images: page 165 left
Courtesy of the Arata Isozaki & Associates: pages 182-183, 183 top, 184-185
Courtesy of the Ricardo Bofill Taller de Arquitectura: pages 186, 187
Courtesy of theChristian Drevet Société d'Architectures: pages 82, 83
Courtesy of the Arthur Erickson Architectural Corporation: page 201
Courtesy of the Kallmann McKinnell & Wood Architects: pages 173, 175
Courtesy of the Museo Civico di Gibellina: page 157 (3rd photo)
Courtesy of the Pei Cobb Freed & Partners Architects LLP: pages 174-175
Courtesy of the Renzo Piano Building Workshop: pages 181, 206, 207
Courtesy of the Albert Viaplana /David Viaplana arqts. S.L.: pages 190, 192 bottom
Courtesy of the West 8 Urban Design & Landscape Architecture: page 204

Acknowledgments

The author would like to thank:
Fulvio Irace, Graziella Leyla Ciagà, Carlo and Mimmi Feraboli

The publisher would like to thank:
Bildarchiv der Österreichischen Nationalbibliothek, Vienna, Ulrike Polnitzky
Ricardo Bofill Taller de Arquitectura, Barcelona, Serena Vergano
Martin Català Roca, Barcelona
Ceschia & Mentil Architetti Associati, Venice
City of Toronto Archives, Andrea Aitken and Sharon Anderson
Comune di Venezia, Ufficio Patrimonio, Simone Bortolato
Didrichsen Art Museum, Helsinki, Maria Didrichsen
Christian Drevet Société d'Architectures, Lyon, Christian Drevet
El Poder de la Palabra, Barcelona-New York, Nina Delgado
Arthur Erickson Architectural Corporation, Vancouver, Nicole Milkovich
Geoffrey Erickson
Hartmann Edition, Paris, Véronique Hartmann
Yasuhiro Ishimoto, Vicki Harris (Laurence Miller Gallery) and Akiko Yamada (Photo Gallery International)
Arata Isozaki & Associates, Tokyo, Takako Fujimoto
JGM - Jenkins/Gales & Martinez Inc., Los Angeles, Sabrina Martin-Edwards
Kallmann McKinnell & Wood Architects, Boston, Clare McParland and Linda Lyman
Musei Capitolini, Rome, Angela Carbonaro
Museo Civico di Gibellina, Tommaso Palermo
Museum of Finnish Architecture, Helsinki, Petteri Kummala
Pei Cobb Freed & Partners Architects LLP, New York, Stephanie Pardue and James Balga
Renzo Piano Building Workshop, Genea, Stefania Canta and Giovanna Giusto
PPS - Project for Public Spaces, New York, Katie Salay
Jean-Baptiste Suet
University of Calgary, Canadian Architectural Archives, Linda Fraser and Karly Sawatzky
Albert Viaplana / David Viaplana arqts. S.L., Barcelona, Patricia de Muga
West 8 Urban Design & Landscape Architecture, Rotterdam, Daphne Schuit